W. E. B. Du Bois
on Asia

Edited by Bill V. Mullen and Cathryn Watson

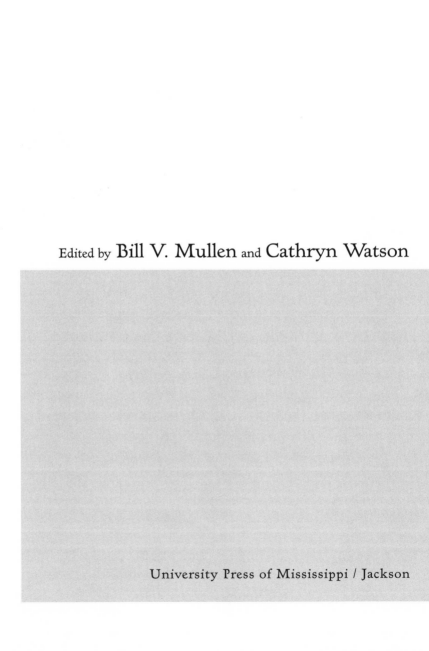

University Press of Mississippi / Jackson

W. E. B. Du Bois on Asia

Crossing the World Color Line

The editors gratefully acknowledge Dr. David Graham Du Bois for permission to reprint the following materials: "India," "The Color Line Belts the World," "The World Problem of the Color Line," "The Negro and Imperialism," "The American Negro and the Darker World," "The Union of Colour," "The Clash of Colour: Indians and American Negroes," "Man Power," "What Japan Has Done," "The Yellow Sea," "China and Japan," "The Color of Asia," "A Chronicle of Race Relations [I]," "A Chronicle of Race Relations [II]," "Prospect of a World Without Racial Conflict," "Nehru," "The Freeing of India," "Gandhi and the American Negroes," "The Colonial Groups in the Postwar World," "Indonesia," "Burma," "Malaya," "Will the Great Gandhi Live Again?," "Our Visit to China," "The Vast Miracle of China Today," and "China and Africa."

The editors gratefully acknowledge International Publishers Co., Inc., for permission to reprint "Asia in Africa."

The editors gratefully acknowledge the National Association for the Advancement of Colored People for permission to reprint "Listen Japan and China" and "Japan and Ethiopia."

www.upress.state.ms.us

The University Press of Mississippi is a member of the Association of American University Presses.

Illustration courtesy of Library of Congress, Prints and Photographs Division

First edition 2005

∞

Library of Congress Cataloging-in-Publication Data

Du Bois, W. E. B. (William Edward Burghardt), 1868–1963.
    W. E. B. Du Bois on Asia : crossing the world color line / edited by Bill V. Mullen and Cathryn Watson.— 1st ed.
        p. cm.
    Includes index.
    ISBN 1-57806-791-X (cloth : alk. paper) — ISBN 1-57806-820-7 (pbk. : alk. paper)
    1. Race relations. 2. Racism. 3. Imperialism. 4. Asia—Race relations. 5. Asia—Social conditions. 6. United States—Race relations. 7. East and West. I. Mullen, Bill, 1959– II. Watson, Cathryn. III. Title.
    HT1521.D732   2005
    305.8—dc22   2005009666

British Library Cataloging-in-Publication Data available

Contents

Introduction

Crossing the World Color Line

The Russo-Japanese war has marked an epoch. The magic of the word "white" is already broken, and the Color Line in civilization has been crossed in modern times as it was in the great past. The awakening of the yellow races is certain. That the awakening of the brown and black races will follow in time, no unprejudiced student of history can doubt.

—W. E. B. Du Bois, "The Color Line Belts the World," 1906

We have been compelled to admit Asia into the picture of future political and democratic power. We can no longer regard Europe as the sole center of the world. The development of human beings in the future is going to depend largely upon what happens in Asia.

—W. E. B. Du Bois, "The World Problem of the Color Line," 1945

Hail, dark brethren
    Of mine,
Hail and farewell!
    I die,
As you are born again,
    Bursting with new life.

—W. E. B. Du Bois, "I Sing to China," 1959

W. E. B. Du Bois's lifelong interest in Asia and the vast body of writing he produced on it are both the least understood and the most neglected aspects of his storied intellectual career. From 1903, when he famously pronounced, in *Souls of Black Folk*, "The problem of the twentieth century will be the problem of the color line," to his death in exile in Ghana in 1963, Du Bois consistently saw Asia as the fraternal twin to African—and African American—struggle for political freedom and cultural self-preservation. In 1914, on the eve of World War I, Du Bois revised his color line trope as a hemispheric index to the world's future. Predicting "a great coming war of Races," Du Bois wrote:

> If . . . men would look carefully around them . . . they would see that the Problem of the Color Line in America instead of being the closing chapter of past history is the opening page of a new era. All over the world the diversified races are coming into close and closer contact as never before. We are nearer China today than we were to San Francisco yesterday.[1]

Well before it was fashionable to do so, Du Bois perceived globalization, national interdependence, and multiple ethnic diasporas as ineluctable elements of the modern world. Black and Asian nations and citizens stood at the crossroads of these phenomena in Du Bois's work. All of the major issues upon which he fixed his critical gaze—race, nationhood, capitalism, labor, gender, imperialism, culture, colonialism—were at one time or another weighed by Du Bois on the basis of events in Asia. In the process, Du Bois spent inordinate intellectual effort which taxed both his expertise and at times political judgment to comprehend and theorize the place of Asia in the modern world. Asian history, economy, culture, political thought, religion, myth, and art were all subjects of his writing and study. Remarkably, given the range of his other, better-known accomplishments, Du Bois's work also offers the most copious canvas for understanding black-Asian exchange of any American or African American intellectual of the twentieth century.

Yet why, thus far, has this element of Du Bois's career been so overlooked? There is as yet a single book-length study to be written of Du Bois's work on Asia. Scholarly articles addressing Du Bois's writings on Japan, China, India, the South Pacific, or the Middle East are rare. Many of the major biographies of Du Bois, including the best ones, gloss or ignore the trips Du Bois made to the Soviet Union, China, and Japan, and tend to neglect the writing he did towards the end of his life in support of China's Communist revolution. There are a host of answers to this omission, I believe. They describe in part the difficulty of summing up the sheer scope and depth of Du Bois's life work. They also speak to a form of critical ethnocentrism, or hemispherism, Du Bois himself worked all his life to disarm. First, Du Bois's identification as the American founder of Pan-Africanism has focused attention on the capacious body of work and writing he did on that subject at the neglect of other elements of his career. From his attendance at the first Pan-African Congress meeting in London in 1900, to his organizing role in the 1945 conference in Manchester, England, Pan-Africanism provided Du Bois a public forum for his ideas and publishing venues for his thought that found no correspondent to his work on Asia. To take but one example: his essay "The African Roots of the War," first published in 1915 and later published in revised form in *Darkwater* (1919), is one of Du Bois's most astute predictive essays about the role of Africa in the movement of twentieth-century European colonialism. Du Bois literally argues that World War I is grounded in interimperialist rivalry rooted in nineteenth-century colonization of Africa. Yet the same essay underscores historical relationships between Africa and Asia as a means of predicting the place of India, China, and the Middle East in the postwar world. Likewise, Du Bois's intimate friendship with Caribbean intellectual and Pan-African activists George Padmore and Ghanian President Kwame Nkrumah, his belated efforts to produce the *Encyclopedia Africana*, and his eventual death-in-exile in Ghana in 1963 have also bent the arc of Du Bois scholarship towards the African trajectory of his career. These notable events have obscured Du Bois's personal relationships to other internationalists like Lala Lajpat Rai, one of the founders of modern Indian nationalism, and Du Bois's generous written support for Sun Yat Sen, Jawa-harlal Nehru, Mao Tse-Tung, and Mahatma Gandhi, the latter perhaps the international leader of the twentieth century with whom Du Bois felt the closest kinship. In total, concentration on Du Bois's Pan-Africanism has occluded Du Bois's Pan-Asianism as well as the ways in which the two were complementary.

Second, Du Bois's most lasting contributions to the canon of African American political thought, most especially his 1903 book *Souls of Black Folk*, his founding and editorship of the NAACP journal *Crisis*, and his collaborative work with U.S. black intellectuals like Paul Robeson on the anticolonial movement, have understandably concentrated much of the attention on the direct impact of Du Bois's political work on the political culture of the United States. In turn, U.S. critics especially have tended to read this work for its grounding in western, European, or otherwise Anglocentric thought at the expense of attention to Asian influence. Important studies of Du Bois by scholars like Ross Posnock, Manning Marable, Arnold Rampersad, and David Levering Lewis have offered copious analysis of the influence of German romanticism, Jamesian psychology, European and American socialism, and other important tenets of western thought on Du Bois's intellectual training.[2] Likewise, biographers and critics have explored in detail how key Du Boisian concepts like "double consciousness" may be understood as reiterations or revisions of European or in some cases Afrocentric ideas. Wilson Jeremiah Moses, in his book *Afrotopia: The Roots of African Popular History*, ventures closest to exploring the place of Asia in Du Bois's thought by examining the influence of eighteenth- and nineteenth-century Egytocentrism and Afrocentrism on Du Bois's early writings on culture, especially.[3] Yet generally speaking, Du Bois's writing on Asia has been overshadowed by the press of events in African-America during his lifetime. During Harlem's Renaissance for example, about which he wrote some of his best remembered essays like "Criteria of Negro Art," Du Bois was simultaneously writing essays on India and China that few readers in his time, and few after, found as compelling or important. Du Bois's best novel, *Dark Princess*, was likewise published at the height of the Harlem Renaissance but in part because of its focus on events outside of the U.S.—Berlin, India, and Japan—has rarely been considered a key text to that movement, even though Du Bois was living in Harlem when he wrote it. Indeed it has only been with the republication of the book by University Press of Mississippi, and a broadened scholarly perspective on international currents flowing through the Renaissance itself, that Du Bois's book has earned renewed critical interest.

Lastly, and perhaps most significant of all, the shadow of American anti-Communism has both obscured and reduced the significance of Du Bois's work on Asia. The official blacklisting of Du Bois that began in 1952 with charges of "alien sedition" by the U.S. state department was coincident with, and in many ways a result of his strong intellectual and political turn to support for Asia in his writing. Du Bois, that is, turned further East as he turned deeper Red, and vice versa. Du Bois wrote several extended adulatory essays and poems on China's cultural revolution at the very height of U.S. animus towards Communism. These pieces, published in places like *Peking Review* and *China Reconstructs* to which few Americans had access, could not have had the same impact of Du Bois's earlier work for *Crisis* on either African-America or the wider public. At the same time, they did not go unnoticed. Fellow African Americans of the 1950s like Paul Robeson and proto-black Nationalists of the period like Robert F. Williams were acutely aware of Du Bois's support for China as an important phase of anticolonial struggle and Afro-Asian unity. When Du Bois died in 1963, his American eulogies often neglected this element of his work while it became central to his legacy in Asian nations. Similarly, and relatedly, much of this work was passed over or obscured by scholars during the Cold War, part of a conscious and unconscious narrowing of Du Bois's legacy. Herbert Aptheker remained attentive to Du Bois's writings on Asia, as he did all else he published, because he was one of the few not to dissent from Soviet or Chinese Communism during the Cold War. And yet the last twenty years of Du Bois's life are literally incomprehensible without some analysis of why he made such a strong turn to support for China's revolution. Explaining it away as a late-in-life delusion or deathbed conversion does Du Bois and Du Bois scholarship the grave injustice of failing to see how this support was in many ways the culminating gesture of a life dedicated in the main to supporting political or cultural causes Du Bois deemed in the best interest of colored people's global liberation. More particularly, it ignores this central theme in Du Bois's life and work: that events in Asia drove much of his political analysis and determined many of the most important positions he took and decisions he made.

It is towards a deeper and more comprehensive understanding of all of these aspects of Du Bois's life and thought that the current volume is dedicated. It is the central argument of *W. E. B. Du Bois on Asia* that few if any of the major aspects of Du Bois's thought and life are understandable without consideration of their relationship to Du Bois's views on Asia. Indeed from the earliest stages of his career, Du Bois himself warned his contemporaries, particularly African American contemporaries, that they neglected the conditions of the Asian world at their own great peril. In 1935, Du Bois wrote, "American Negroes have in their own internal color lines the plain shadow of a caste system. For American Negroes have a large infiltration of white blood and the tendency to measure worth by the degree of this mulatto strain." Thus black Americans had much to learn from Asia, Du Bois argued, especially India. He implored both parties to see their interests as commingled in order to work towards mutual liberation:

> The problem of the Negroes thus remains a part of the worldwide clash of color. So, too, the problem of the Indians can never be simply a problem of autonomy in the British commonwealth of nations. They must always stand as representative of the colored races—of the yellow and black peoples as well as the brown—of the majority of mankind, and together with the Negroes they must face the insistent problem of the assumption of the

white peoples of Europe that they have a right to dominate the world and especially so to organize it politically and industrially as to make most men their slaves and servants.[4]

This passage is emblematic of what might be called Du Bois's Asian methodology. As with his assessment of Africa and African-America, Du Bois's analysis of Asia's place in the world emerged directly alongside of, and organically from, a simultaneous assessment of race, nationality, culture, and empire. Indeed it is possible to construct something like an Afro-Asian timeline or chronology of global events which forced Du Bois to see the black and Asian worlds as straddling the hemispheric color line (see Appendix I). These included the rise of Pan-Asianism and Pan-Africanism after 1885, both of which Du Bois vigorously supported; the earliest stirrings of anticolonialism, including the Boxer Rebellion and the formation of the Indian National Congress; the defeat of Russia by Japan in their 1904 war, an event Du Bois heralded in prophetic terms. During World War I, Du Bois was a tireless combatant against "yellow peril" and anti-Asian hysteria fomented by American racial theorists like Madison Grant and Lothrop Stoddard. In his important aforementioned 1919 essay "The African Roots of the War," published in revised form in *Darkwater*, Du Bois imagined Asia as one with the African "all-black Mother," a figure of colored solidarity meant to stave off genocidal ideas about the "rising tide" of color against white world supremacy. In 1928, Du Bois published *Dark Princess*, an allegory of efforts of black and Asian radicals to resist colonialism and build national and international movements during and after the war. During the 1930s and 1940s, Du Bois was by far the most advanced and tireless American proponent of both African and Asian decolonization. He made supportive visits to both Japan and China in 1936 and 1937 at the height of their Civil War; guaranteed the presence of Asian state leaders at the 1945 Pan-African Congress in Manchester, England, and wrote passionate, hagiographic essays on

Mahatma Ghandi and Jawa-harlal Nehru. India's struggle for independence he described as the one of the "greatest events of the modern world" next only to the Russian Revolution. After 1945, Du Bois also directed extraordinary public support in particular to Ghana and China's revolutions. In 1959, he visited the country and offered China as the singular model for African nations seeking independence to follow. Indeed inspired almost wholly by China's example, Du Bois joined the Communist Party of the United States just before his exile to Ghana and death in 1963.

Yet Du Bois was also, as in many things, a fierce autodidact on Asia. He neither spoke nor wrote a single Asian language. His travel in Asia was limited to Russia, Japan, and China, in part due to Cold War restrictions on his passport after 1952. His most copious and scholarly essay on Asia, "Asia in Africa," was a patchwork borrowing heavily from both established and marginalized scholars on African and Asian antiquity. Thus, Du Bois's writing on Asia is marked by what I have called elsewhere a form of Afro-Orientalism: a combination of passionate intellectual desire to wed African American political interest and African American support to Asian destiny, and an at times incomplete, romanticized, or willful analysis of events there. Afro-Orientalism may best be understood as the complex effort to undo a form of white supremacy—Orientalism—which Du Bois understood threatened black Americans as well as Asians, while fostering a colored unity that, owing to geographical, cultural, and physical distance, was difficult to achieve in practice. To this notion adhered an analysis of black and Asian workers as the fulcrum of modern capitalist exploitation and the greatest single force of hope for overthrowing it. For Du Bois, Afro-Asian unity was a racial, cultural, and economic imperative necessitated by what he perceived as the central dynamic of the twentieth century: white and western domination of colored people. Afro-Orientalism, in this light, may be understood as a counterdiscourse to a modernity which simultaneously threatened blacks and Asians with perpetual subjugation, exploitation, and division and yet, dialectically, made both visible and urgent the need for Afro-Asian unity. This, Du Bois's most underappreciated theme, courses through and provides unity to a vast body of writing on economy and culture, race and colonialism, imperialism and diaspora in which Asian culture, economy, and society play a recurring, central role.

At the same time, Du Bois's profound desire for black-Asian unity in the face of white supremacy rarely dulled his interest in supporting Asian national cultures and causes even when it was threatened with eclipse by what he didn't know or wouldn't acknowledge about them. For example, Du Bois referred to China as the "riddle of the universe" after visiting for the first time and made the most profound political misjudgment of his career in his delinquent tolerance for Japanese imperialism. To his credit, Du Bois was influenced in the direction of support for Japan by the complex of events of the 1930s. Germany's anti-Semitic rise, China's woeful struggles for economic stability, and Civil War and worldwide depression in capitalist countries persuaded Du Bois, as he wrote in selections included here, that a colored nation's ascent—even into authoritarianism—was necessary to stay and contain the effects of western colonialism and imperialism. Here Du Bois shared the urgent political interest of some members of the black working-classes in the U.S. who looked to a vibrant Japanese nationalism, as Gerald Horne, Ernest Allen, Jr., and Vijay Prashad have noted, as a star to which to hitch their own antiwhite supremacist politics. Afro-Orientalism includes this ambition and its contradictions. It articulates both Du Bois's analysis of Asia as part of a developing dialectical materialism, on one hand, as well as at times a contradictory tendency towards nationalism, essentialism, or what might be called culturalist readings of history.[5] In this, as in many things, Du Bois was inclusive of the twentieth century's most vital competing intellectual strands.

Indeed Du Bois's penchant for racial romanticism, rooted in his infatuation with nineteenth-century views of race and culture, profoundly colored his writing on Asia and provides a fascinating and not yet fully explicated subject in his work. Crude theories of "bloodties" between Japanese and Chinese clouded his analysis of those countries' military conflict during the 1930s; influenced especially by nineteenth-century European race theorists and Afrocentrists, Du Bois produced sensational historiography on Asia, mystifying and elevating its place in antiquity in order to raise it to a formidable position for black Americans in the twentieth century. Du Bois's self-described "favorite" book, *Dark Princess*, is likewise a mildly, or wildly, depending upon one's reading, Orientalist affair. Subtitled "A Romance," it depicts a heavily eroticized political relationship between a black Pullman porter and a royal Indian Princess. Though clearly a brave and brazen critique of antimiscegenation hysteria, and a fascinating rendering of radical love, *Dark Princess*, in its rendering of Princess Kautilya, bespeaks a tendency in Du Bois to both "feminize" Asia in his corpus of writing and to transform it into an object of utopian political and cultural fantasias. Du Bois likewise frequently assigned Asia a distinctive place as a marker of culture, an inheritance of his argument in *Souls of Black Folk* that the "kingdom of culture" was a necessary plateau to which subordinated or subaltern groups should aspire. In its entirety, then, Du Bois's Afro-Orientalism should be understood as part of an important and admirable lifelong struggle to seek multiple affiliations and connections between the black and Asian worlds that historical circumstances, racist ideology, miscegenation hysteria, geography, and certainly the U.S. government conspired against.

Perhaps most emblematic of the brilliance, acumen, complexity, and contradictions of Du Bois's work on Asia are in fact the columns he wrote during the 1930s for the *Pittsburgh Courier* struggling to assess, as he put it in writing, "What Japan Has Done?" As noted earlier, Japan's rise to power presented Du Bois with a flourish of hope for a colored nation's challenge to western imperialism. Later, confronted with evidence of Japanese atrocity especially in China, Du Bois formulated a provocative critique that ultimately blamed

Japanese imperialism on western slavery, colonialism, and the encroachment of racist and imperialist ideals onto Asia by the West. The complex negotiations of these ideas are on display in pieces collected here in Section II of the book. Indeed the trajectory of *W. E. B. Du Bois on Asia* is meant to suggest what might be called "stagist" development in Du Bois's thought triggered by events in Asia. Part I, "The Color Line Belts the World," preserves in its title the dominant racialist trope to which Du Bois wedded much of his early domestic and international analysis. Part II, "Darkwater Rising: Japan and the Color of Imperialism," signals the trauma and crisis to this racialized conception caused by realignment of world power and the influence of fascism, Communism, and imperialism. To take one example, in his descriptions of imperialism of the 1940s, Du Bois described anti-Communism as a "color curtain" that hung for thousands of years between the developed and developing, white and colored worlds. Communism, anti-Communism, colonialism, and anti-imperialism were the recombinatory ingredients of Du Bois's writings on Asia (and Africa) during and after the 1930s. They left the vocabulary and ideas of his earlier work both revised and changed. Part III of *W. E. B. Du Bois on Asia* marshals some of the more complex articulations of this change, sampling some of Du Bois's longer essays and assessments of Asia, global politics, and imperialism in a section entitled "World War II and the Anticolonial Turn." Finally, part IV, "The East Is Red: Revolutions and Resolutions," offers journalistic, essayist, and jeremiadic representations of Du Bois's firm and at times ecstatic hope that Communism, Socialism, or some combination, under the inspired leadership of revolutionary China, might become the pandemic force of change in the colored world.

Tracing Du Bois's career from an Asian angle also foregrounds a number of elements of Du Bois's career obscured by neglect of this aspect of his work. One of those is the central place of Asia in Du Bois's lifelong development into Marxism and Communism.

Though he first gave serious study to the ideas of Marx and Engels while a student in Berlin in the 1890s, it was the emergence of Indian socialism at the turn of the century that first drew his enthusiasm for Marxism as a counterforce to the spiritual and material history of the West. U.S. socialism had by 1915 already earned a checkered place in Du Bois's eyes. The failure of American socialists, laborites, and especially the American Federation of Labor to repudiate racism and make room for black (and other colored) workers persuaded him that Marxism was destined to replicate Eurocentrism's political and philosophical exclusions. India's example of collective colored struggle sustained and ignited, Du Bois's radical and ultimately more dialectical analysis of World War I as a war permanently cleaving the globe into white and colored, exploiter and exploited. Indeed a signal event in this period was Du Bois's friendship with the aforementioned Lala Lajpat Rai, a staunch proponent of Indian anticolonial nationalism exiled to the U.S. in 1916. Du Bois and Rai become fast friends and correspondents. Du Bois showed Rai drafts for critical comment on *Dark Princess* and wrote flattering reviews of his work in *Crisis*. Rai was no Communist, but during the 1920s he influenced Du Bois to consider India's radical nationalist movements, including Communist-influenced movements of exiles in Berlin, as the possible linchpins of a new postwar alignment of power. Du Bois in turn paid careful attention to events like the Soviet Cominterns of 1922 and 1928, especially the Eastern Conference at Baku and the formation of the Soviet University grandiosely titled "Toilers of the East." These events, designed to develop and apply Soviet policy to the question of national liberation in Asia, served as sympathetic allegorical backdrop to the internationalist maneuverings in *Dark Princess*. They also inspired Du Bois's more generous appraisals of American Communist enterprises like the efforts of Communist Unemployed Councils in cities like Chicago, and the formation of the National Negro Congress, a heavily Communist-influenced front organization crucial to help building the Popular Front in the U.S.

Subsequent to World War I, Du Bois commonly described the problem of the twentieth century not just as a problem of the color line, but of the distribution of wealth and resources between and among the colored peoples of the world. His book *Darkwater*, published in 1919, included penetrating analysis of the relationship between the war and colonialism in Africa. Throughout the 1920s and 1930s, Du Bois wrote repeatedly on the relationship between black workers struggles in the U.S., the conditions of labor in India and China in particular, and the potential for colored workers' revolutions in both spheres of the world. In *The World and Africa*, his monumental and decisive book on the need to destroy imperialism, Du Bois argued that only a method of analysis that addressed this issue—including, if necessary, a Marxist method—could begin to alleviate the suffering and brute reality of masses of dark workers' lives. Du Bois thus came to understand "proletarianization" primarily as the process of western capitalism's interpellation of black, brown, and Asian workers in the advance of capitalism. In 1944, Du Bois published "The Colonial Groups in the Postwar World." "Capitalism has benefited mankind," he wrote there, "but not in equal proportions. It has enormously raised the standard of living in Europe and even more in North America":

> But in the parts of the world where human toil and natural resources have made the greatest contribution to the accumulation of wealth, such parts of the earth, curiously enough, have benefited least from the new commerce and industry. This is show by the plight of Africa and India today.[6]

This assessment became the focal point of the last twenty years of his life. Du Bois insisted that only colored labor and colored nations could lead the world out from its impasse of unequal development and racial exploitation. White workers were welcome to join their struggle, though Du Bois remained, to the end of his life, suspicious about the psychological and spiritual fringe benefits of what he called famously in *Black Reconstruction* the "wages of whiteness."

This made all the more important and compelling the place of Asia in his search for pan-ethnic unity. Du Bois was utterly convinced that white supremacy was a bedrock of capitalism and imperialism, and that only—and perhaps not until then—when colored workers of the world united did a chance for any alternative future to it exist.

W. E. B. Du Bois on Asia also sheds important light on the vexed relationship in Du Bois's work between race and culture. More than has been acknowledged by critics of his work, Afrocentrism, Egyptocentrism, and nativist racial romanticism infused Du Bois's writings on culture. In "Asia in Africa," for example, Du Bois's argument that "the Negroid people of Asia have played a leading part in our (black) history" was assembled from catholic evidence of Dravidian Buddhism drawn from nineteenth-century texts like G. Massey's *A Book of the Beginnings*. Du Bois's early forays into debates about Afro-Asiatic antiquity relied upon cultural sources—music, religion, and the visual arts most pronouncedly. Indeed as was characteristic of his writing even on contemporary Asia, "cultural" signs of national identity were the foregrounded texts of his critical interpretations of Asian societies. Traveling in Japan and China, for example, Du Bois was quite literally an occidental tourist, ingesting Shinto Buddhism, panoramic vistas, and historical monuments under the watchful eyes of sympathetic tourguides who had as much to profit by Du Bois's favorable impression as did he. Thus the long arc of his writing on Asia reveals an odd manner of imperial eyeballing. Particularly in his latter essays and poems, written during his birthday visit to China in 1959, Du Bois often deployed an ecstatic or prophetic voice when describing the wonders of the Asian world, a kind of revolutionary sublime that seems to find its form, literally, in lyricism. Du Bois avoids the excessive mysticism and mythologization that has beset other Afrocentric renderings of Afro-Asian antiquity, but even in the essays on China written near the end of his life one sees the vestiges of a racial romanticism that—perhaps another aspect of his Afro-Orientalism—was far more marked in his writing on Asia than on Africa or African-America.

In addition, critical assessment of the entire corpus of his work on Asia requires some application of the taxonomic and interpretive tools that sometimes go by the name postcolonial theory. For one, Du Bois's writings on Asia well predate the canon of work often considered "postcolonial." He is the first African-American to articulate what we would call after Fanon a "wretched of the earth" reading of colonialism, and the first to draw extensive connection between the conditions of African Americans in the U.S. and their darker brothers around the world. Du Bois also forecasts postcolonial studies interest in the questions of internal and external colonialism, liminality, or what Du Bois called "double consciousness," Orientalism, and the relationship between northern and southern hemispheres. Like the planners of the 1955 Bandung Conference in Indonesia, often seen as postcolonial history's moment of birth, Du Bois understood colonialism to be the central cultural and political event of his lifetime, marking everything before and after, fulfilling Europe's Enlightenment dreams, producing resistance wherever it went, determining what was necessary and sufficient for people to live all over the globe. This motivated not only his need to travel and ultimately choose exile, but his insistence that all forms of isolationism—political, culture, literary—were delusions. In short, Du Bois was a diasporic thinker from the get-go. Like his compatriot Richard Wright, who likewise turned to Africa and Asia as the subject of his discourses on empire, Du Bois evinced what Paul Gilroy calls "negative loyalty" to the West as he worked his way to an epistemology of liberation for the colored world. Du Bois in Asia, like Wright in Indonesia, or Baldwin in Switzerland, makes a fascinating case study of the black internationalist neither entirely at home in nor outside the world.

Equally important, Du Bois's writings on Asia occupy a special niche in the literature of transnationalism and transnational theory. Du Bois's travels and writings on Asia are important markers of what has become a central figure in literatures of black diaspora, namely the questing cosmopolitan. Particularly during his excursions to

China and Japan in the 1930s and 1950s, Du Bois desperately sought a placeholder outside the U.S. for his tentative new allegiances and leanings to Marxian Communism, Maoism, anticolonialism, on one hand, and his voracious and expanding interest in rapidly developing political and cultural phenomenon barely ascertainable to most Western eyes: Islam, or what Du Bois often called anachronistically "Mohameddism," Buddhism, Confucianism, and the Cultural Revolution. Du Bois's historical writings on the spread of Islam, for example, make interesting counterpoint and antecedent to the later discoveries of Malcolm X. At the same time, his exclamatory proclamations of faith in China's uneven and tragically incomplete revolution of the 1950s, to whose deficits Du Bois turned a blind eye, anticipate much of the fervor with which 1960s black nationalists like the Revolutionary Action Movement and Black Panther Party would take up the cause of Chinese and Vietnamese liberation. In this regard, Du Bois is in many ways the intellectual (if not political) American counterpart to philosopher of revolution Ho Chi Minh: a global, diasporic seeker of revolutionary wisdom. Du Bois's incorporation of Asian anticolonial struggle and Cultural Revolutionary enthusiasm remained mediated to the end of his life by simultaneous fidelity to Pan-Africanist principles, basic commitment to civil rights tenets in the U.S., his own stripe of Hegelian, or dialectical idealism, and a social democratic impulse that determined much of the "shape" of his own improvised radicalism.

Finally, this presentation of Du Bois's writings on Asia holds promise for scholars in Asian and Asian-American studies seeking to fill gaps in the corpus of U.S. expression on twentieth-century Asian history. Interestingly, Du Bois's academic and essayistic writings on Asia predate the formation of Asia studies—the first American "area studies" programs developed in the U.S. Indeed it is interesting to note how especially during the 1940s Du Bois's anticolonial analysis of South Asia and East Asia in particular clashed with state department—sponsored area studies research, much of which was meant to consolidate prodemocratic, anticommunist policy, and so consider how this, too, helped lead to Du Bois losing his appointment at Atlanta University in 1944, and later losing his visa to travel abroad. More positively, Du Bois's essays reprinted here on Burmese, Malaysian, and Indonesian independence movements offer rare commentaries on struggles that were primarily the purview of Asian area studies scholars in their time, and rarely the purview of American or African American readers. Du Bois's writings on Gandhi and Nehru likewise suggest fresh new routes for exploring the long relationship between African-American and Asian pacifisms more commonly understood through the figures of Bayard Rustin and Martin Luther King, Jr. Du Bois's support for Japan and China during the 1930s and 1940s likewise may be understood as counterpart to his condemnation of Japanese internment during World War II in the U.S. and his fierce debates and attacks on American Orientalist scholars like Lothrop Stoddard. Indeed, scholars of Asian and Asian American history may generally find new readings of Orientalism available in Du Bois as well as new lines of dissent against its pernicious influence on the U.S. and Asia. Finally, serious attention by Asian and Asian-American scholars to Du Bois's autodidacticism, especially his interpretations of Asian antiquity, would help situate that work as part of a longer effort to popularize and explain Asian culture in the U.S.

Seeing the long arc of Du Bois's writings on Asia thus generally recenters, or recasts African American intellectual life in this century as the profoundly internationalist affair that it is. As critics like Nikhil Singh, William Maxwell, Kate Baldwin, James Smethurst, Brent Edwards, and Penny von Eschen have shown,[7] a central theme in African American literature and political life of the twentieth century, the alleged century of the "color line," has been the real and imagined line of cross-racial, international solidarity that, as Du Bois put it in 1906, "belts the world." Du Bois's articles appeared in the Indian nationalist magazine *Aryan Path* published in Bombay; *Peking Review* and *China Pictorial* published in Beijing; the *New*

Times and *Problems in Anthropology* published in Moscow; *Women of the Whole World* published in Berlin; *Bulletin of the World Peace Council* published in Vienna. Vietnam was a somewhat conspicuous absence from his commentary of the 1950s. Smitten with China, Du Bois seemed not to completely apprehend the depth and scope of Vietnam's national liberation struggle. And yet, precisely at a time in U.S. Cold War history when it was career and political suicide, Du Bois championed Asian independence movements, Communist and non-Communist, as the most hopeful curb on the rise of new American imperial power in the postwar world. Though restrictions on his travel visa prevented him from attending, Du Bois also noted that the 1955 Bandung Conference of twenty-nine decolonizing African and Asian heads of state was a watershed of history; his speech commemorating the event later is included in part III of this collection. The Bandung conference, organized by among others India's Nehru and Ghana's Kwame Nkrumah to demonstrate Afro-Asian resolve and solidarity during the 1950s tide of decolonization, was in fact the culmination of a dream Du Bois first articulated in *Dark Princess*. There Princess Kautilya, forecasting a revolutionary future, predicts the "colored world goes free in 1952." Later, in 1959, in a speech entitled "China and Africa," included here, Du Bois readily predicted that only when American workers—and Europeans—learned the valuable lessons of China's selfless Communism could workers around the world unite in common cause. Likewise, Africa's decolonizing fortunes, and chances for independence, relied on the degree to which they could learn from China: "China is flesh of our flesh, and blood of your blood," wrote Du Bois.

> China is colored and knows to what a colored skin in this modern world subjects its owner. But China knows more, much more than this: she knows what to do about it. She can take the insults of the United States and still hold her head high. She can make her own machines, when America refuses to sell her American manufacture, even though it hurts American industry, and throws her workers out of jobs. China does not

need American nor British missionaries to teach her religion and scare her with tales of hell. China has been in hell too long, not to believe in a heaven of her own making. This she is doing.[8]

Though neither Bandung nor China's Communist Revolution fulfilled the promise of Afro-Asian solidarity to which Du Bois devoted much of his life, a subject for another day and another book, *W. E. B. Du Bois on Asia* provides evidentiary affirmation that Du Bois's "call" throughout his life work did earn the Asian world's response. To take but two final examples past and present obscured to U.S. readers by time, distance, and world events: in September 1963, *Shijie Wenxue* (*World Literature*), a Chinese literary journal published in Beijing, occasioned Du Bois's passing with a commemorative issue dedicated to his life. The issue appeared a mere month after the March on Washington. It included Du Bois's own poem, "Ghana Calls," Sie Ping-hsin's "To Mourn for the Death of Dr. W Du Bois," poems by the celebrated African-American writer Margaret Walker, and a short story by South African writer Ronald Segal. Later in Beijing, David Graham Du Bois, the son of W. E. B. and Shirley Graham Du Bois, helped to establish a Council of the China-Du Bois Study Centre. The Centre operates to this day. These events are among the symbolic footprints that reveal how Du Bois himself crossed the color line and that the color line did not stand still. The Asian tracks he left across the terrain of Asia, the U.S., and African American literature and thought are ubiquitous. This volume hopes to make those tracks more visible still and to encourage appreciation of still another W. E. B. Du Bois, one whose giant steps into Asia may yet comprise a great leap forward for our understanding of how to analyze, live, and challenge the next century's color lines.

Notes

1. W. E. B. Du Bois, "The World Problem of the Color Line." *Manchester Leader*. Nov. 16, 1914.

2. See David Levering Lewis *W. E. B. Du Bois: Biography of a Race*, a two-volume study (New York: Henry Holt, 1993 and 2000); Ross Posnock, *Color & Culture: Black Writers and the Making of the Modern Intellectual* (Cambridge: Harvard University Press, 1998); Arnold Rampersad, *The Art and Imagination of W. E. B. Du Bois* (Cambridge: Harvard University Press, 1979). Other important life studies of Du Bois include Gerald Horne, *Black & Red: W. E. B. Du Bois and the Afro-American Response to the Cold War, 1944–1963* (Albany: State University of New York Press, 1986), and Manning Marable, *W. E. B. Du Bois: Black Radical Democrat* (Boston: Twayne, 1986). See also Hazel Carby's *Race Men* (Cambridge: Harvard University Press, 1998).

3. See Wilson Moses, *Afrotopia: The Roots of African Popular History* (Cambridge: Cambridge University Press, 1998). Other examples of illuminating scholarship on Du Bois and Asia include Vijay Prashad, *The Karma of Brown Folk* (Minneapolis: University of Minnesota Press, 2000) and *Everybody Was Kung Fu Fighting: Afro-Asian Connections and the Myth of Cultural Purity* (Boston: Beacon Press, 2001), especially chapter 2, "The American Ideology," pp. 37–69 ; Kate Baldwin, *Beyond the Color Line and the Iron Curtain: Reading Encounters Between Black and Red, 1922–1963* (Durham: Duke University Press, 2002); Gerald Horne, *Race War! White Supremacy and the Japanese Attack on the British Empire* (New York: NYU Press, 2004); Arnold Rampersad, Chapter 10, "*Dark Princess*," in *The Art and Imagination of W. E. B. Du Bois* (Cambridge: Harvard University Press, 1976).

4. Untitled. Published as "India" in "Some Unpublished Writings of W. E. B. Du Bois" in *Freedomways*, V. 5, n. 1 (Winter 1965): pp. 115–17.

5. For more on Afro-Orientalism see my "W. E. B. Du Bois, *Dark Princess*, and the Afro-Asian International" in *Left of the Color Line: Race, Radicalism, and Twentieth-Century Literature of the United States* (Durham: University of North Carolina Press, 2003), pp. 87–106 and *Afro-Orientalism* (Minneapolis: University of Minnesota Press, 2004). For more on African American attraction to Japanese imperialism and nationalism see Horne and Prashad (above) and Ernest Allen, Jr., "When Japan Was 'Champion of the Darker Races': Satokata Takahashi and the Flowering of Black Messianic Nationalism," *The Black Scholar*, V. 24, n. 1 (Winter 1994): pp. 23–46. "Japan the Champion of the Colored Races?" refers to the title of a 1938 pamphlet published by the Negro Commission National Committee of the Communist Party of the United States. The pamphlet, published by Workers Library Publishers, Inc., and prepared by among others Party members Cyril Briggs, James W. Ford, and Harry Haywood, argued that Japanese imperialism and fascism were the "enemy" of African Americans even while underscoring the Popular Front position of the CPUSA that African Americans had a stake in "democracy." During World War II A. Philip Randolph also cautioned that "Any Negro who believes that the victory of Japan will advance the cause of the Negro people is living in a fool's paradise." See "Editorial: Pro-Japanese Activities Among Negroes," *The Black Worker*, V. 7, n. 209 (Sept. 1942): p. 4.

6. "Colonialism, Democracy, and Peace after the War." In *W. E. B. Du Bois, Against Racism: Unpublished Essays, Papers, Addresses, 1887–1961.* Ed. Herbert Aptheker (Amherst: University of Massachusetts Press, 1985), p. 233.

7. Among the best books describing efforts towards Black internationalism are Penny Von Eschen's *Race Against Empire* (Ithaca: Cornell University Press, 1996); Brent Edwards, *The Practice of Diaspora: Literature, Translation and the Rise of Black Internationalism* (Cambridge: Harvard University Press, 2003); William Maxwell's *Old Left, New Negro* (New York: Columbia University Press, 1999); Nikhil Pal Singh's *Black Is a Country: Race and the Unfinished Struggle for Democracy* (Cambridge: Harvard University Press, 2004) and James Smethurst's *The New Red Negro* (New York: Oxford University Press, 1999). An especially important contribution to scholarship on Afro-Asian connections is the *positions: east asia cultures critique* special issue *The Afro-Asian Century*, Ed. Andrew Jones and Nikhil Pal Singh, (Durham: Duke University Press, 2003). Standard works on the subject of black diaspora include Paul Gilroy's *The Black Atlantic: Modernity and Double Consciousness* (Cambridge: Harvard University Press, 1993) and Carol Boyce Davies, *Black Women, Writing and Identity: Migrations of the Subject* (New York: Routledge, 1994).

8. "China and Africa," in W. E. B. Du Bois, *The World and Africa: An Inquiry into the Part Which Africa Has Played in World History* (New York: International Publishers, 1972), p. 314.

PART I

The Color Line
Belts the World

Du Bois's earliest writing on race was significantly imprinted by nineteenth-century raciological thinking. It was also rooted in notions of geography, culture and race. As Wilson Moses has demonstrated, nineteenth-century U.S. race theorists, most notably Edward Wilmont Blyden and Alexander Crummell, conceived of the Afro-Asiatic world of antiquity as a discrete cultural sphere outside of Europe.[1] For Blyden and Crummell, Egypt and North Africa comprised part of the greater ancient Orient. Black culture in antiquity was the distillation of nonwhite and non-European sources. These sources, the apex of a great black civilizational past, had been laid low by modernity, including colonialism and the slave trade. The modern "color line" was thus also a culture line that endeavored to erase the contributions of Afro-Asia to world culture.

Du Bois eventually made this argument his own in his essay "Asia in Africa." Yet as with all else, Du Bois filtered the history of black thought on Asia through multiple contemporary lenses. This first section offers a sampling of these essays, scattered across a broad swath of his career. It begins with "Asia in Africa" as his most sustained historical analysis of Asia's place in antiquity and its relationship to

1

the African world. "Africa in Asia" was the culmination of several threads in Du Bois's work: his documentary interest in the early years of Pan-Asianism, especially in Japan, India, and China; an ongoing scholarship on the history of Africa; an abiding interest in Asian religion, particularly the role of Buddhism and Hinduism in Asian cultural and political formations; and an engagement with modern-day Orientalist theory as it emerged in full force in the U.S. around the period of World War I with the publication of books like Lothrop Stoddard's *Rising Tide of Color Against White Supremacy* and Madison Grant's *The Passing of the Great Race*. Against these books, which merged eugenics theory, white supremacy, and a malicious crosshatch of anthropological evidence of Asian and black inferiority, Du Bois began to muster counterevidence of the glories of Afro-Asian antiquity. Du Bois sustained this interest by staying abreast of nineteenth- and early twentieth-century scholarship on antiquity and the formation of racial classification. Charles Tauber, G. Massey, Edward Balfour, Joseph P. Widney, Alfred T. Butler, and Marcel Dieulafoy were among the nineteenth- and early twentieth-century Anglo-European scholars Du Bois invokes in the essay. In this seminal work of scholarship on black, Indian, and Egyptian place in the transformation of the ancient world, Du Bois also made use of insights from Jawaharlal Nehru's *Autobiography* (1940) and *Glimpses of World History* (1942); and both Harry H. Johnston's *The Negro in the New World* and the pioneering work of J. A. Rogers found place in the essay's literature review. "Asia in Africa" appeared in the revised and expanded edition of *The World and Africa*, Du Bois's monumental 1946 book. In many ways it anchors the two central arguments of the book. The first is that black-Asian exchange was a veiled shaping source of the ancient world. Du Bois here anticipates more full-blown modern-day Afrocentric arguments by scholars like Molefi Asante and Martin Bernal's controversial *Black Athena* scholarship tracing the Afro-Asian roots of Greco-Roman culture. The second primary argument of *The World and Africa* is that Western capitalism and imperialism have laid low the once great empires of Africa and Asia and thus necessitated their rise against colonialism. This dialectical conception, what Wilson Moses calls Du Bois's "Afrocentric Marxism," enunciates creative tensions in his writing on Asia redolent throughout his career. "Asia in Africa" is essential reading for anyone attempting to understand Du Bois's place in this lineage of black thought.

Other selections in this section comprise signal moments when Du Bois attempted to imagine and reimagine his color line thesis as linked to and dependent upon an inclusion of the Asian world. It represents the secular cast of his political analysis that often accompanied his essays on Afro-Asian religiosity and culture. "The Color Lines Belts the World," first published in *Collier's Weekly* on October 20, 1906, asserts that the "color" line and race itself are in emergent crisis produced directly out of what he calls "the policy of expansion." The essay cites English, French, Dutch, Italian, Portugese, and U.S. territorial reach at the turn of the century as calling the "hegemony of civilization" into question: "The color question enters into European imperial politics and floods our continent from Alaska to Patagonia," he writes. Significantly, the event occasioning Du Bois's essay was the "awakening of the yellow races" in the aftermath of the Russo-Japanese war, an event Du Bois predicted would result in the "awakening of the brown and black races." The essay is the first dramatic revision of Du Bois's 1900 color line thesis. It indicates how rapidly he was assimilating the role of the post-1898 dawning of U.S. imperialism into a theory of world empire, and how processes of colonization in North America were for Du Bois both mirror and continuation of longer European schemes. The essay forecasts a century of acquisition and domination with men and women of color as the prospective sacrificial lambs or progenitors of a foreboding future.

In 1914, in "The World Problem of the Color Line," Du Bois revised his "color line" trope yet again, attaching it to the growing racial hysteria coterminous with the outset of World War I. Here

Du Bois cites rising nationalist race prejudice and xenophobia as a toxic cocktail of new global prejudices: "It has been suggested more than once that Christianity was not to apply in these human relations and that the world must revert to the ethics of the club and claw in a great coming war of Races." The essay is significant as a moment in which Du Bois apprehended for the first time the pernicious inclusion of U.S. blacks as targets of Orientalist discourse. Thus the essay succinctly predicts that black American fortunes—"the Negro problem"—are invariably hitched to the fate of the darker races the world over. This is the theme, too, of what might be called a pedagogical essay by Du Bois first written in 1936 or 1937. Titled "India," the essay makes an explicit case that black and South Asian destinies are invariably linked. The world caste system mandates, and the interdependent systems of slavery and colonialism make it imperative for Du Bois, that African Americans and Indians dispel the ignorance, myth, and miseducation that obscures their mutual understanding. The essay is one of Du Bois's more explicit appeals to black Americans to "read" globally. It also signals an early attempt to theorize colonial linkages between subalterns in the U.S. and Asia, an especially urgent task for Du Bois in the wake of the Soviet experiment and nascent anticolonial stirrings of the 1920s. "India" forecasts Du Bois's growing obsession with figures like Gandhi, whose work against apartheid had already drawn his attention, and the systemic movement of capital in the direction of colonial empire and eventually world war.

The complication and deepening analysis of these events is captured in a pair of more advanced, retrospective essays that stand as two of Du Bois's most complex and important analyses of Asia as a point of reference for understanding the fate of colored people under Western capitalist empire. "The Negro and Imperialism" was delivered as a radio address over station WEVD in New York City on November 15, 1944. The title of the essay is misleading. The occasion for the essay is Du Bois's outrage that the preliminary conference of the United Nations Organization at Dumbarton Oaks failed to include direct representation of colonized countries. He cited in particular China's exclusion, and linked it to the League of Nations refusal to recognize Japan's proposal for a "racial-equality declaration among nations" during World War I. The essay predicts the UN exclusion will lead to disaster. "The working people of the civilized world will thus largely be induced to put their political power behind imperialism, and democracy in Europe will continue to impede and nullify democracy in Asia and Africa." The essay synthesizes Du Bois's analysis of the effects of nineteenth-century imperialism and twentieth-century racial supremacy doctrine with an urgent critique of the U.S. as a tool of empire. In 1951, Du Bois, Paul Robeson, New York City Councilman Ben Davis, William Patterson, and others signers delivered their "We Charge Genocide: The Crime of Government Against the Negro People" petition to the U.N. claiming that its policies were tantamount to a license to kill for western imperialist countries. The roots of that famous pamphlet lie in this 1944 essay.

The section closes with an important and rarely read essay, "The American Negro and the Darker World." The essay has both intellectual gravity and symbolic weight for the theme of this book. The essay was first published as a six-page pamphlet in 1957 by the National Committee to Defend Negro Leadership, a Communist-influenced organization formed to combat accusations of anti-Americanism against figures like Du Bois and Paul Robeson (who provided a foreword for the original). The pamphlet is a comprehensive assessment of the historical emergence of western imperialism, from colonial sugar to plantation cotton, from Napoleonic dynasty to the Third Reich. The focus of the essay, though, is the crushing blows delivered by world capitalism against the world's working classes, and the added impact of racism on workers of color. The essay enumerates the role of Pan-African Congresses from 1900 to 1945 to stem the tide of white supremacist colonialism, but, echoing

Lenin, and disclosing his increasing application of historical materialism, the essay encourages American Negroes to respond by turning to Asia: "We can learn about China and India and the vast realm of Indonesia rescued from Holland. . . . We can realize by reading, if not in class-room, how socialism is expanding over the modern world." Significantly, the essay was written and delivered as a speech given by Du Bois at the second anniversary of the Bandung Conference held in Harlem on April 30, 1957. The essay attempts to apply the lessons of Bandung, and the wider struggles of anticolonialism, to African Americans, and to place African American historical struggles in the context of what has become known to us now as the "Bandung Era."

Notes

1. Wilson Jeremiah Moses, *Afrotopia: The Roots of African Popular History* (Cambridge: Cambridge University Press, 1998).

Publication History for Part I

"India." Originally published in *Freedomways*, V. 5, n. 1 (Winter 1965). Reprinted in *Against Racism: Unpublished Essays, Papers, Addresses, 1887–1961*. Ed. Herbert Aptheker. Amherst: University of Massachusetts Press, 1985, pp. 115–17.

"Asia in Africa." Chapter IX in *The World and Africa*. New York: International Publishers, 1965, pp. 176–200. Orig. published 1947.

"The Color Line Belts the World." *Collier's Weekly*, V. 28 (Oct. 20, 1906): p. 20. Reprinted in the *Public*, V. 9 (Oct. 27, 1906): pp. 708–9.

"The Negro and Imperialism." Radio Address WEVD 1944. Published in *W. E. B. Du Bois Speaks: Speeches and Addresses, 1920–1963*. Ed. Phillip Foner. New York: Pathfinder Press, 1972, pp. 150–60.

The American Negro and the Darker World. Brooklyn: New York, National Committee to Defend Negro Leadership, 1957. 5 pp. Introduction by Paul Robeson. Published in *Pamphlets and Leaflets*, by W. E. B. Du Bois. Ed. Herbert Aptheker. White Plains, NY: Kraus-Thompson Publishing Company, 1986, pp. 329–33.

India

To most Indians, the problem of American Negroes—of twelve million people swallowed in a great nation, as compared with the more than three hundred millions of India—may seem unimportant. It would be very easy for intelligent Indians to succumb to the widespread propaganda that these Negroes have neither the brains nor ability to take a decisive part in the modern world. On the other hand, American Negroes have long considered that their destiny lay with the American people; that their object was to become full American citizens and eventually lose themselves in the nation by continued intermingling of blood. But there are many things that have happened and are happening in the modern world to show that both these lines of thought are erroneous. The American Negroes belong to a group which went through the fire of American slavery and is now a part of the vast American industrial organization; nevertheless, it exists as representative of two hundred or more million Negroes in Africa, the West Indies and South America. In many respects, although not in all, this group may be regarded as the leading intelligentsia of the black race and no matter what its destiny in America, its problems will never be settled until the problem of the relation of the white and colored races is settled throughout the world.

India has also had temptation to stand apart from the darker peoples and seek her affinities among whites. She has long wished to regard herself as "Aryan" rather than "colored" and to think of herself as much nearer physically and spiritually to Germany and England than to Africa, China or the South Seas. And yet the history of the modern world shows the futility of this thought. European exploitation desires the black slave, the Chinese coolie and the Indian laborer for the same ends and the same purposes, and calls them all "niggers."

If India has her castes, American Negroes have in their own internal color lines the plain shadow of a caste system. For American Negroes have a large infiltration of white blood and the tendency to measure worth by the degree of this mulatto strain.

The problem of the Negroes thus remains a part of the worldwide clash of color. So, too, the problem of the Indians can never be simply a problem of autonomy in the British commonwealth of nations. They must always stand as representatives of the colored races—of the yellow and black peoples as well as the brown—of the majority of mankind, and together with the Negroes they must face the insistent problem of the assumption of the white peoples of Europe that they have a right to dominate the world and especially so to organize it politically and industrially as to make most men their slaves and servants.

This attitude on the part of the white world has doubtless softened since the [First] World War. Nevertheless, the present desperate attempt of Italy in Ethiopia and the real reasons back of the unexpected opposition on the part of the League of Nations, show that the ideals of the white world have not yet essentially changed. If now the colored peoples—Negroes, Indians, Chinese and Japanese—are going successfully to oppose these assumptions of white Europe, they have got to be sure of their own attitude toward their laboring masses. Otherwise they will substitute for the exploitation of colored by white races, an exploitation of colored races by colored men. If, however, they can follow the newer ideals which look upon human labor as the only real and final repository of political power, and conceive that the freeing of the human spirit and real liberty of life will only come when industrial exploitation has ceased and the struggle to live is not confined to a mad fight for food, clothes and shelter; then and only then, can the union of the darker races bring a new and beautiful world, not simply for themselves, but for all men.

Asia in Africa

The connection between Asia and Africa has always been close. There was probably actual land connection in prehistoric times, and the black race appears in both continents in the earliest records, making it doubtful which continent is the point of origin. Certainly the Negroid people of Asia have played a leading part in her history. The blacks of Melanesia have scoured the seas, and Charles Taüber makes them inventors of one of the world's first written languages: thus "this greatest of all human inventions was made by aborigines whose descendants today rank among the lowest, the proto-Australians."[1]

The ethnic history of India would seem to be first a prehistoric substratum of Negrillos or black dwarfs; then the pre-Dravidians, a taller, larger type of Negro; then the Dravidians, Negroes with some mixture of Mongoloid and later of Caucasoid stocks. The Dravidian Negroes laid the bases of Indian culture thousands of years before the Christian era. On these descended through Afghanistan an Asiatic or Eastern European element, usually called Aryan.

The *Rig Veda*, ancient sacred hymns of India, tells of the fierce struggles between these whites and blacks for the mastery of India. It sings of Aryan deities who rushed furiously into battle against the black foe. The hymns praise Indra, the white deity, for having killed fifty thousand blacks, "piercing the citadel of the enemy" and forcing the blacks to run out in distress, leaving all their food and belongings. The blacks under their renowned leader Krishna, that is, "The Black," fought back with valor. The whites long held the conquered blacks in caste servitude, but eventually the color line disappeared

9

before commerce and industry, intermarriage, and defense against enemies from without.

In the Gangetic region caste disappeared. The whites enlisted in the service of the blacks and fought under Negro chiefs. In the famous battle of the Ten Kings, one of the leading Aryan chiefs was a Negro. Nesfield said: "The Aryan invader, whatever class he might belong to, was in the habit of taking the women of the country as wives, and hence no caste, not even that of the Brahman, can claim to have sprung from Aryan ancestors."[2] Today some of the Brahmans are as black and as flat-nosed as the early Negro chiefs. Max Müller said that some Brahmans are "as black as Pariahs."[3]

The culture of the black Dravidians underlies the whole culture of India, whose greatest religious leader is often limned as black and curly-haired. According to Massey: "It is certain that the Black Buddha of India was imaged in the Negroid type. In the black Negro God, whether called Buddha or Sut-Nahsi we have a datum. They carry their color in the proof of their origin. The people who first fashioned and worshipped the divine image in the Negroid mould of humanity must, according to all knowledge of human nature, have been Negroes themselves. For blackness is not merely mystical, the features and hair of Buddha belong to the black race and Nahsi is the Negro name. The genetrix represented as the Dea Multi-mammia, the Diana of Ephesus, is found as a black figure, nor is the hue mystical only, for the features are Negroid as were those of the black Isis in Egypt."[4]

Of the thirty apostles who took Buddhism to China, ten are represented as yellow, ten brown, and ten black. The Indian blacks, mingling with the straight-haired yellow Mongoloids, tended to have straighter hair along with their dark color than Africans, although this was not true in the case of the island Negroes.

According to Balfour: "Ethnologists are of the opinion that Africa has had an important influence in the colonization of Southern Asia, of India, and of the Easter Islands in time prior to authentic history or tradition. The marked African features of some of the people in the extreme south of the Peninsula of India, the Negro and Negrito races of the Andamans and Great Nicobar, the Semang, Bila, and Jakun of the Malay Peninsula, and the Negrito and Negro, Papuan and Malagasi races of the islands of the Indian Archipelago, Australia, and Polynesia, indicate the extent which characterizes their colonization. . . . The spiral-haired Negro race seem to have preceded the lank-haired brown race. . . . When we consider the position of India between the two great Negro provinces, that on the west being still mainly Negro, even in most of its improved races, and that on the east preserving the ancient Negro basis in points so near India as the Andamans and Kedah, it becomes highly probable that the African element in the population of the Peninsula has been transmitted from an archaic period before the Semitic, Turanian, and Iranian races entered India and when the Indian Ocean had Negro tribes along its northern as well as its eastern and western shores. . . . Perhaps all the original population of southern Arabia, and even of the Semitic lands, generally was once African."[5]

Widney has said: "They [the Negroes] once occupied a much wider territory and wielded a vastly greater influence upon earth than they do now. They are found chiefly in Africa, yet traces of them are to be found through the Islands of Malaysia, remnants, no doubt, of that more numerous black population which seems to have occupied tropical Asia before the days of the Semites, the Mongols, and the Brahminic Aryan. Back in the centuries which are scarcely historic, where history gives only vague hintings, are traces of a widespread, primitive civilization, crude, imperfect, garish, barbaric, yet ruling the world from its seats of power in the valley of the Ganges, the Euphrates, and the Nile, and it was of the Black races. The first Babylon seems to have been of a Negroid race. The earliest Egyptian civilization seems to have been Negroid. It was in the days before the Semite was known in either land. The Black seems to have built up a great empire, such as it was, by the waters of the Ganges before Mongol or Aryan. Way down under the mud and slime of the beginnings . . . is the Negroid contribution to the fair superstructure of modern civilization."[6]

H. Imbert, a French anthropologist, who lived in the Far East, has said in *Les Negritos de la Chine*: "The Negroid races peopled at some time all the south of India, Indo-China, and China. The south of Indo-China actually has now pure Negritos as the Semangs, and mixed as the Malays and the Sakais. . . . In the first epochs of Chinese history, the Negrito type peopled all the south of this country and even in the island of Hai-Nan, as we have attempted to prove in our study on the Negritos, or Black Men, of this island. Skulls of these Negroes have been found in the island of Formosa and traces of this Negroid element in the islands of Liu-kiuto the south of Japan. In the earliest Chinese history several texts in classic books spoke of these diminutive blacks; thus the Tcheu-Li composed under the dynasty of Tcheu (1122–249 B.C.), gives a description of the inhabitants with black and oily skin. . . . The Prince Liu-Nan who died in 122 B.C., speaks of a kingdom of diminutive blacks in the southwest of China."

Additional evidence of Negroes in China is given by Professor Chang Hsing-land in an article entitled, "The Importation of Negro slaves to China under the "T'ang Dynasty, A.D. 618–907": "The Lin-yi Kuo Chuan (Topography of the Land of Lin-yi) contained in Book 197 of the Chiu T'ang Shu (Old Dynastic History of T'ang) says: 'The people living to the south of Lin-yi have woolly hair and black skin.'" Chinese folklore speaks often of these Negroes, he says, and mentions an empress of China, named Li (A.D. 373–397), consort of the Emperor Hsiao Wu Wen, who is spoken of as being a Negro. He adds that according to the writings of a later period—the seventh to the ninth century—Negro slaves were imported into China from Africa.[7]

According to Professor Munro, one of the foremost students of Japanese life and culture: "The Japanese are a mixture of several distinct stocks—Negritos-Mongolian. . . . Breadth of face, intraorbital width, flat nose, prognathism, and brachycephaly might be traced to the Negro stock.[8]

The Asiatic and African blacks were strewn along a straight path between tropical Asia and tropical Africa, and there was much racial intermingling between Africa and western Asia. In Arabia particularly the Mongoloids and Negroids mingled from earliest times. The Mongoloids invaded North Africa in prehistoric times, and their union with the Negroids formed the Libyans. Later there was considerable commerce and contact between the Phoenicians of North Africa, especially Carthage, and the black peoples of the Sudan.

Speaking of the mixture that went on in this area between Elamite black and Aryan white, Dieulafoy has said: "The Greeks themselves seemed to have known these two Susian races, the Negroes of the plains and the Scythian whites of the mountains. Have not their old poets given to the direct descendants of the Susian, Memnon, the legendary hero who perished under the walls of Troy, a Negro father, Tithon, and a white, mountain woman as mother—Kissia? Do they not also say that Memnon commanded an army of black and white regiments? 'Memnon went to the succor of Priam with ten thousand Susians and ten thousand Ethiopians.'. . . I shall attempt to show to what distant antiquity belongs the establishment of the Negritos upon the left bank of the Tigris and the elements constituting the Susian monarchy. . . . Towards 2300 B.C., the plains of the Tigris and Anzan-Susinka were ruled by a dynasty of Negro kings.

"The coming of this dynasty of Medes corresponded perhaps to the arrival in the south of an immense Scythian invasion. Pushed back by the black Susians after having taken possession of the mountains, the whites poured into the plains of the Tigris and remained master of the country until the time when Kudur Nakhunta subdued Chaldea and founded Anzan-Susinka. He added to the territory of the blacks—Nime, Kussi, Habardip—all the mountainous districts once inhabited by the whites of the Scythian race."[9]

Herodotus, who visited this region in the fifth century B.C., mentioned the dark skins of the people. He called them Ethiopians, but said their hair was straighter than those of the western Ethiopians, who had woolly hair. The Elamites, however, seemed rather to have belonged to the more Negroid stock of the west; their hair, as seen on the monuments, is short and woolly. "The Elamites," said Sir Harry Johnston, "appear to have been a Negroid people with kinky hair and to have transmitted this racial type to the Jews and Syrians. There is curliness of the hair, together with a Negro eye and full lips in the portraiture of Assyria which conveys the idea of an evident Negro element in Babylonia. Quite probably the very ancient Negro invasion of Mediterranean Europe (of which the skeletons of the Alpes Maritimes are vestiges) came from Syria and Asia Minor on its way to Central and Western Europe."[10]

Professor Toynbee also says, "The primitive Arabs who were the ruling element of the Omayyad Caliphate called themselves 'the swarthy people' with a connotation of racial superiority, and their Persian and Turkish subjects, 'the ruddy people,' with a connotation of racial inferiority, that is to say, they drew the distinction that we draw between blonds and brunets but reversed the value."[11]

Carthage especially traded with the Sudan for gold dust, ostrich feathers, and ivory in exchange for textiles, cloth, copper, and beads. Often the Carthaginians settled among the Negroes and the Negroes among them. As a result the horse became known in the Sudan, textiles were made from cotton, and gold was gathered and worked. The glass industry was born and spread. The Libyans, or Berbers, were descendants from the populations of North Africa which consisted of an Asiatic element that came in prehistoric times and mixed with the Negroids. From these mixed races came the Sudan stone houses and the cemented wells and the spread of cattle-raising and gardening.

The whole population becomes darker and darker toward the south, until it merges into the blacks of the Sudan. The divisions, especially the political units—Tripoli, Tunisia, Algeria, and Morocco— have no anthropological significance and do not correspond to any ethnic division. There are many striking groups: the Negroid Tuareg, or people of the Veil; the Tibu, or rock people. Negroids with mixed Mongoloid or Caucasoid blood; the dark Fulani, scattered all over North Africa from the Upper Niger to the Senegal and forming often the dominant political power in the lands toward the coast.

Mohammedanism arose in the Arabian deserts, starting from Mecca which was in that part of the world which the Greeks called Ethiopia and regarded as part of the African Ethiopia. It must from earliest time have had a large population of Negroids.

The two greatest colored figures in the history of Islam are Bilal-i-Habesh (Bilal of Ethiopia) and Tarik-bin-Ziad: "Bilal-i-Habesh was Mohammed's liberated slave and closest friend to whom he gave precedence over himself in Paradise. The Prophet liberated all his slaves, and they were all well-known figures in the early Islamic history. He adopted as his own son another Negro, Zayd bin Harith, his third convert, who rose to be one of his greatest generals. Later, to show his regard for Zayd, he took one of Zayd's wives, the beautiful Zainab, as his own. But Bilal stands out in greatest relief. Apart from his services in the cause of Islam, it was through him that the Moslems decided to use the human voice instead of bells to call the Moslems to prayer. He had evidently a marvelous voice and was the first who called for prayers in Islam.

"Tarik-bin-Ziad also was a slave and became a great general in Islam and was the conqueror of Spain as the commander of the Moorish Army which invaded Spain. Jebel-u-Tarik (the mount of Tarik), that is, Gibraltar, is named after him. One of the greatest Turkish classics is called 'Tarik-bin-Ziad' and has him as its hero. It was written by Abdul-Hak-Hamid, our greatest poet (alive though eighty-four) and equals any tragedy of Corneille. I do hope that some time the biographies of these great figures will be written in English."[12]

The Mohammedans organized for proselyting the world, overthrew Persia, and took Syria and eventually Egypt and North Africa from the Eastern Roman Empire. They went east as far as India and west to Spain, and eventually the Golden Horde, as the Russian Mongols had come to be called, became followers of Islam and thus religious brothers of the Mohammedan Arabs.

The Arabs brought the new religion of Mohammed into North Africa. During the seventh century they did not migrate in great numbers. Spain was conquered not by Arabs, but by armies of Berbers and Negroids led by Arabs. Later, in the eleventh century, another wave of Arabs came, but the number was never large and their prestige came from their religion and their language, which became a *lingua franca* for the peoples north and south of the Sahara. The total substitution of Arabian for Berber or Negro blood was small.

Anyone who has traveled in the Sudan knows that most of the "Arabs" he has met are dark-skinned, sometimes practically black, often have Negroid features, and hair that may be almost Negro in quality. It is then obvious that in Africa the term "Arab" is applied to any people professing Islam, however much race mixture has occurred, so that while the term has a cultural value it is of little ethnic significance and is often misleading.

The Arabs were too nearly akin to Negroes to draw an absolute color line. Antar, one of the great pre-Islamic poets of Arabia, was the son of a black woman; and one of the great poets at the court of Harun-al-Rashid was black. In the twelfth century a learned Negro poet resided at Seville.

The Mohammedans crossed the Pyrenees in A.D. 719 and met Charles Martel at Poitiers; repulsed, the invaders turned back and settled in Spain. The conflict for the control of the Mohammedan world eventually left Spain in anarchy. A prince of the Omayyads arrived in 758. This Abdurahman, after thirty years of fighting, founded an independent government which became the Caliphate of Cordova. His power was based on his army of Negro and white

Christian slaves. He established a magnificent court and restored order, and his son gave protection to writers and thinkers.

Eventually rule passed into the hands of a mulatto, Almanzor, who kept order with his army of Berbers and Negroes, making fifty invasions into Christian territory. He died in 1002, and in a few years the Caliphate declined and the Christians began to reconquer the country. The Mohammedans looked to Africa for refuge.

In the eleventh century there was quite a large Arab immigration. The Berbers and some Negroes by that time had adopted the Arab tongue and the Mohammedan religion, and Mohammedanism had spread slowly southward across the Sahara.[13]

The invasions of the eleventh century were launched in 1048 by the Vizier of Egypt under the colored Caliph Mustansir. Each man was provided with a camel and given a gold piece, the only condition being that he must settle in the west. In two years they pillaged Cyrenaica and Tripoli and captured Kairwan. The invaders for the most part settled in Tripoli and Tunis, while their companions pressed on westward into Morocco. This exemplifies the process of arabization in North Africa, and it was to a large extent a reflex from the invasion that had most to do with the arabization of the Nile valley. It is thus responsible for much of the present-day distribution of the "Arab" tribes of the Sudan.

The Arabs invaded African Egypt, taking it from the Eastern Roman Emperors and securing as allies the native Negroid Egyptians, now called Copts, and using Sudanese blacks, Persians, and Turks in their armies. They came in 639 under Amr-ibn-el-Asr, partly as friends of Egyptians against the tyranny of the Eastern Roman Empire, partly even as defenders of the heretical Coptic Church. It must be remembered that they were related by blood and history to the Negroid peoples. One of Mohammed's concubines was a dark curly-haired Coptic woman, May; and Nubians from the Sudan took frequent part in these wars. Alexandria surrendered in 642, and ten years later the Arabs invaded Nubia and attacked Dongola crying, "Ye people of Nubia, Ye shall dwell in safety!"[14]

For two centuries from 651 there were ninety-eight Mohammedan governors of Egypt under Caliphs of Medina, Damascus, and Bagdad. The Copts, representing the majority of the Egyptians, for the most part submitted to this rulership, but the black Nubians continued to be unruly and even came to the defense of the Copts. In 722 King Cyriacus of Nubia marched into Egypt with one hundred thousand soldiers and secured release of the imprisoned Coptic patriarch. There is an intriguing story of a black virgin whom the Mohammedans had seized and who promised them an unguent to make them invulnerable. To prove it she put it on her own neck, and when the Arab soldier swept his sword down upon her, her head fell off as she had intended.[15]

The change from the Omayyad to the Abasid Caliphs took place in Egypt peacefully in the middle of the eighth century. By 832 Egypt had become almost entirely Mohammedan, by conversion of the Copts through economic and social pressure. In 852 the last Arab governor ruled in Egypt, and in 856 the Turks began to replace the Arabs and to favor the Copts. There was much misrule, and from 868 to 884 Ahmed-ibn-Tulun, a Turkish slave, ruled. The Berga people of the Sudan refused further tribute of four hundred slaves annually and revolted in 854; the army of Ali Baba, "King of the Sudan," led the revolt, but spears and shields strove against mail armor and Arab ships, and failed.

We know that in 850 four hundred black East Africans had been enrolled in the army of Abu'l Abbas, ruler of Bagdad, and that they rose in revolt with a Negro, called "Lord of the Blacks," at their head. In 869 the Persian adventurer, Al Kabith summoned the black slaves to revolt, and they flocked to his side in tens of thousands. In 871 they captured Basra and for fourteen years dominated the Euphrates delta. When Masudi visited this country fourteen years later, he was told that this conquest by famine and sword had killed at least a million people.

Syria was annexed to Egypt in 872, and from that time until the eleventh century Egypt, Syria, Palestine, and Mesopotamia form one realm, more or less closely united. When Syria was first annexed, Egypt ruled from the Euphrates to Barka and Aswan, and the famous black cavalry of ten thousand or more took part in the conquest. In 883 the Zeng Negroes of East Africa revolted, and some settled in Mesopotamia. The Tulum dynasty finally ended in 905, and there were thirty years of unsettled rule in Egypt under the suzerainty of weak caliphs. From 935 to 946 Ikshid was governor of Egypt.

He was succeeded by a black Abyssinian eunuch, Abu-l-Misk Kafur, "Musky Camphor," for whom Ikshid named a celebrated garden in Cairo. Kafur was a clever man of deep black color with smooth shiny skin, who had been guardian of the sons of Ikshid. He read history and listened to music and was lavish with his vast wealth. Daily at his table there were served two hundred sheep and lamb, seven hundred and fifty fowls, and a thousand birds and one hundred jars of sweetmeats. He attracted men of learning and letters and began an era of art and literature which placed Egypt as a cultural center next to Bagdad, Damascus, and Cordova.[16] The poet Muttanabi praised him as "The Moon of Darkness."

Kafur ruled Egypt for twenty-two years, from 946 to 968; he was regent for nineteen years, but the two sons of Ikshid who were nominally on the throne were playboys without power. Kafur ruled three years alone, from 965 to 968. He conquered Damascus and Aleppo and incorporated Syria under Egyptian rule. Trouble arose from time to time in Syria, while in Egypt there were earthquakes, bad Nile seasons, and a Nubian revolt. Nevertheless, in general good order was maintained. He died in 968 and was succeeded by a child, then by the Caliph Hoseyn, and finally by Moizz.

The Shiites or Fatimids from Morocco, under the man who called himself the Mahdi, now began to war on Egypt and conquered it. They sent an embassy to George, King of Nubia; reconquered Syria and became rich with gold and jewelry, ivory and silk. By the middle of the twelfth century the Mohammedan empire included North Africa, Syria, Sicily, and Hejaz; Turkish slaves and Sudanese troops held the empire.

Moizz was helped by Killis, a Jew who had been Kafur's righthand man; and had a bodyguard of four thousand young men, white and black. By the help of Negro troops another Syrian revolt was quelled. Then came the reign of mad Hakim and finally Zahir.

Zahir ruled Egypt from 1021 to 1026. His wife was a black Sudanese woman, and after the death of her husband largely influenced the rule of her son, who came to the throne in 1036 and ruled until 1094, the longest reign in the dynasty. This son, M'add, took the name of Mustansir and is regarded as the best and ablest of the rulers of his time. He loved and encouraged learning and had a library of a hundred and twenty thousand volumes. The Black Dowager, who had great influence over him, sailed the Nile in her silver barge and imported additional Negro troops from the south, until Mustansir had in his escort fifty thousand black soldiers and swordsmen, twenty thousand Berbers, ten thousand Turks, and thirty thousand white slaves. For years all Upper Egypt was held by black regiments.

Mustansir had enormous wealth, including his celebrated golden mattress. Makrizi described his jewels, gold plate, and ivory. Cairo consisted at this time of twenty thousand brick houses; there was art in pottery and glass work, and a beautiful "Lake of the Abyssinians." Mustansir had difficulties with Syria and nearly lost his power in 1068; his library was destroyed and the Black Dowager had to flee to Bagdad for sanctuary. Through the aid of Bedar, his prime minister, he regained power and restored Syria to Egyptian rule.

Then the Seljukian Turks appeared. They subdued Persia, captured Bagdad, and attacked Syria. Jerusalem was captured in 1071, and this became the excuse for the European Crusades which began in 1096, two years after Mustansir died. The Europeans took Jerusalem in 1099 and later seized most of Syria, but Egypt, with the aid of the black veterans of Mustansir's former army, eventually defeated Baldwin in 1102. From 1169 to 1193 Saladin, the Kurd, ruled Egypt and the East.

After Saladin's accession, black Nubian troops attacked Egypt, and the rebellion continued for many years. Gradually Saladin asserted his power in Nubia, and peace was made with the African Zeng in Mesopotamia. Mesopotamia had been ruined by the Mongols, and Cairo now became the greatest cultural center in the Orient, and indeed in the world, from 1196 to 1250. Saint Francis of Assisi preached there in 1219, and world trade centered in Alexandria.

Artists flocked to Egypt from Asia Minor. Men of culture lived at court, poets and writers. The Thousand and One Nights stories were collected. Indian stories and European romances were combined with Egyptian materials. A companion collection of poems made at this time were those of Antar-bin-Shaddad. He was born about A.D. 498, the son of a black slave girl, Zebbeda, and of Shaddad, a nobleman of the tribe of Abs. Antar is famous. One of his works is found as the sixth poem of the Mo'allaqat—the "golden verses"—which are considered in Arabia the greatest poems ever written. The story is that they were hung on the Ka'bah at the Holy Temple at Mecca so that all the pilgrims who came there might know them and do obeisance to them. The Mo'allaqat belongs to the first school of Arabian poetry—to the "Gahilieh"—"time of ignorance." The Antar poem belongs to the time of the war of Dahis, and, like the five poems which preceded it in the epic, it lauds the victors of the battlefield, describes the beauties of nature, and praises the camel of the desert. The main theme, however, is love.

Rimski-Korsakov's Symphony *Antar*, with its wealth of barbaric color and oriental fire has been deservedly popular. The libretto is drawn from the voluminous work known as *The Romance of Antar*, which was published in Cairo in thirty-two volumes and has been translated in sections from the Arabic by various scholars. There are two editions of the work—one known as the *Syrian Antar*, the other as the *Arabian Antar*. The abridged work was first introduced to European readers in 1802; a translation was made and issued in four books by Terrick Hamilton in 1819. The *Romance* is a companion piece to the *Arabian Nights* and is a standard Arabian work. The seemingly numberless tales that are incorporated in *The Romance of*

Antar are traditional tales of the desert that were retold and preserved by Asmai during the reign of Harun-al-Rashid.

As autocratic power grew among the Mohammedans, a number of religious and political malcontents migrated down the eastern coast of Africa. They filtered through for a number of centuries, not as conquerors, and they were permitted to live and trade in limited areas and mingled and intermarried with the black Bantu. An Arab settlement was made about A.D. 684 under a son-in-law of Mohammed. Then came another migration in 908, and many of the Arabs wandered inland. Cities were established and soon were trading with the gold-mining peoples of Sofala. Masudi, an Arab geographer, visited this part of Africa in the tenth century and described the gold trade and the kingdom of the Waklimi. Marco Polo, writing in 1298, described the island of Madagascar and Zanzibar as peopled with blacks.

There are indications of trade between Nupe in West Africa and Sofala on the East Coast, and certainly trade between Asia and East Africa dates back earlier than the beginning of the Christian era. Asiatic traders settled on the East coast, and by means of mulatto and Negro merchants brought Central Africa into contact with Arabia, India, China, and Malaysia.

Zaide, great-grandson of Ali, nephew and son-in-law of Mohammed, was banished from Arabia. He passed over to Africa and formed settlements. His people mingled with the blacks, and the resulting mulatto traders, known as the Emoxaidi, seem to have wandered as far south as the equator. Other Arabian families came over on account of oppression and founded the towns of Magadosho and Brava, both not far north of the equator. The Emoxaidi, whom the later immigrants regarded as heretics, were driven inland and became the interpreting traders between the coast and the Bantu. Some wanderers from Magadosho came into the port of Sofala and there learned that gold could be obtained. This led to a small Arab settlement at that place.

Seventy years later, and about 150 years before the Norman conquest of England, certain Persians settled at Kilwa in East Africa, led by Hasan-ibn-Ali, who was the son of a black Abyssinian slave mother, and accompanied by his own six sons.

Ibn Batuta, who was acquainted with Arab life on the Mediterranean coast and at Mecca in the fourteenth century, was surprised by the wealth and civilization of East Africa. Kilwa he describes as "one of the most beautiful and best built towns." Mombasa is a "large" and Magadosho an "exceedingly large city."

Duarte Barbosa, visiting the coast ten years later, described Kilwa as "a Moorish town with many fair houses of stone and mortar, with many windows after our fashion, very well laid out in streets, with many flat roofs. The doors are of wood, well carved, with excellent joinery. Around it are streams and orchards and fruit-gardens with many channels of sweet water. . . . And in this town was great plenty of gold, as no ships passed to or from Sofala without coming to this island." Of the Moors, he continued: "There are some fair and some black: they are finely clad in many rich garments of gold and silver in chains and bracelets . . . and many jewelled ear-rings in their ears." Mombasa, again, is "a very fair place, with lofty stone and mortar houses, well lined in streets. . . . Their women go very bravely attired."[17]

It is probable that Chinese ships traded directly with Africa from the eighth to the twelfth centuries. When the Portuguese came they found the Arabs intermarried and integrated with the Bantu and in control of the trade.

One of the most astonishing developments in Africa was the rule of the Mameluke slaves in Egypt for six centuries, from 1193 to 1805. There has been no exact parallel to this in history, and yet students have neglected this period with singular unanimity. The Mamelukes were white slaves bought by the thousands in the Balkans, Greece, Turkey, and the Near East. They were used mainly as soldiers and shared in the conquests of Islam and especially in the capture and holding of the Nile valley. At first they were auxiliary troops under strong and ambitious sultans, several of whom were of Negro descent. Then at the time of the Mongols and Christian Crusades, the Mamelukes, organized by groups of hundreds, began to choose their own chiefs and even raised them to the sultanate. Usually such sultans ruled but short periods, averaging five years. Strong men, like Saladin, held the Mamelukes in control and imposed their policies upon them. Other such powerful rulers were Bibars, who became sultan in 1260; and Kala'un, 1272, whose "Golden Age" was praised by Machiavelli. But gradually the level of culture declined, and instead of the literature and art of Saladin came the brawling, raping, and thieving of ignorant demagogues.

At first these white slaves served side by side with black Sudanese, and even under Negroid rulers. But as the Egyptian sultans tried in vain to conquer Nubia and the south, the Mamelukes found themselves in opposite camps, and white slave rule with few Negroids prevailed in the north, while in the south the Negroes stubbornly held their ground down to the nineteenth century.

The contrast between this white slavery and black American slavery was striking. It involved no inborn racial differences, and because of this Nordic historians have neglected white slavery and tied the idea of slavery to Negroes. The difference between the two groups of slaves was clear: the white slaves, under leadership like that of the colored Mustansir and Saladin the Kurd, opened the way to civilization among both white and black. Had it not been for the attack on this culture by the heathen East and Christian West, the flowering of civilization in Africa might have reached great heights and even led the world.

Napoleon Bonaparte explained the difference between slavery in the East and West:

"These countries were inhabited by men of different colors. Polygamy is the simple way of preventing them from persecuting one another. The legislators have thought that in order that the whites be not enemies of the blacks, the blacks of the whites, the copper-colored of the one and the other, it was necessary to make them all members of the same family and struggle thus against a penchant of man to hate all that is not like him. Mohamet thought that four women were sufficient to attain this goal because each man could have one white, one black, one copper-colored, and one wife of another color. . . .

"When one wishes to give liberty to the blacks in the colonies of America and establish a perfect equality, the legislator will authorize polygamy and permit at the same time a white wife, a black one, and a mulatto one. Then the different colors making part of the same family will be mixed in the opinion of each. Without that one would never obtain satisfactory results. The blacks would be more numerous and cleverer and they would hold the whites in abasement and vice versa.

"Because of the general principle of equality that polygamy has established in the East there is no difference between the individuals composing the house of the Mamelukes. A black slave that a bey had bought from an African caravan became katchef and was the equal of a fine white Mameluk, native of Circassia; there was no thought even of having it otherwise.

"Slavery has never been in the Orient what it was in Europe. The customs in this respect have remained the same as in the Holy Scriptures; the servant marries with the master. In Europe, on the contrary, whoever bore the imprint of the seal of slavery remained always in the last rank. . . ."[18]

According to W. G. Palgrave: "Negroes can without any difficulty give their sons and daughters to the middle or lower class of Arab families, and thus arises a new generation of mixed race. . . . Like their progenitors, they do not readily take their place among the nobles or upper ten thousand; however, they may end by doing even this in process of time; and I have myself, while in Arabia, been honoured by the intimacy of more than one handsome 'Green-man' (mulatto) with a silver-hilted sword at his side and a rich dress on his dusky skin but denominated Sheik, or Emeer, and humbly sued by Arabs of the purest Ishmaelitish or Kahtanic stock. . . . All of this was not by Act of Parliament but by individual will and feeling."[19]

There arose numbers of cases of ruling blacks and mulattoes in the Near East. Nedjeh, a Negro slave, and his descendants ruled Arabia from 1020 to 1158. Again in 1763 Abbas, called "El Mahdi," black, thick-lipped and broad-nosed, ruled Yemen.

The Crusades and Mongols distracted the paths of leaders and left Africa and the Middle East to the ravages of the leadership of the degenerate Mamelukes of the eighteenth century. The black slaves taken to America became after a short period of hesitancy part of a new system of industry. They were chained to hard labor, kept in ignorance, and given no chance for development. Their one goal became freedom, and the Maroons were the nearest counterpart to the Mamelukes. Toussaint in Haiti was the first successful black sultan of the West. Byano and Palmares cleared his way.

There were twenty-five sultans of the Bahrite Mamelukes dynasty; among them was Bibars, who restored Syria to Egypt and attacked the Negroes of the Sudan between 1272 and 1273. Nubia regained its independence in 1320, and there was strife between Nubia and Egypt in 1366, 1385, and 1396. Nubia became practically independent after 1403.

Most scientists agree that the modern Beja are nearest the Egyptian type. Ibn Batuta described them in the fourteenth century. "After fifteen days' travelling we reached the town of Aydhab, a large town, well supplied with milk and fish; dates and grain are imported from Upper Egypt. Its inhabitants are Bejas. These people are black-skinned; they wrap themselves in yellow blankets and tie headbands about a finger-breadth wide around their heads. They do not give their daughters any share in their inheritance. They live on camels' milk and they ride on Meharis (dromedaries). One-third of the city belongs to the Sultan of Egypt and two-thirds to the King of the Bejas, who is called al-Hudrubi. On reaching Aydhab we found that al-Hudrubi was engaged in warfare with the Turks (i.e., the troops of the Sultan of Egypt), that he had sunk the ships and that the Turks had fled before him."[20]

A new dynasty of the Circassian Mamelukes reigned in Egypt from 1382 to 1517 and included twenty-three sultans. Literature and architecture still were cultivated, but there was license and fighting and slave purchases of Mongolians.

Nizir ruled from 1310 to 1341 in Egypt and exchanged embassies with the Mongols of Kepchak, with the Syrians, with the kings of Yemen and Abyssinia, and with West Africa, as well as with the emperors at Constantinople and the kings of Bulgaria.

Africans later were imported into India. King Rukn-ud-din-Barbak, who ruled at Gaur from 1459 to 1474, possessed eight thousand African slaves and was the first king of India to promote them in large numbers to high rank in his service. In 1486 these slaves rebelled, killed Fath Shah, and set their leader on the throne with the title Barbah Shah. Another African, Indil Khan, remained loyal to Fath and, returning from a distant expedition, killed Barbah and accepted the crown under the title of Saif-ud-din-Firuz. Firuz quelled the disorders of the kingdom and restored the discipline of the army. He was succeeded in 1489 by Fath Shah's young son under a regency exercised by another African; but before a year was out still another Negro, Sidi Badr, murdered both child-king and regent and usurped the throne. He reigned three years. In 1493 he was killed at the head of a sortie against rebel forces that were besieging Gaur, and with his death this remarkable Negro regime in Bengal came to an end. An Asiatic from the Oxus country was elected to the throne, and one of his first acts was to expel all the Africans from the kingdom. The exiles, many thousands in number, were turned back from Delhi and Jaunpur and finally drifted to Gujarat and the Deccan, where the slave trade had also created a considerable Negro population.[21]

In the fourteenth century Islam in the West had been shorn of its outposts in Spain and Sicily, but in the East had been extended into India and Malaysia. It had beaten back the Crusaders, but nevertheless signs of weakness appeared. For two centuries Islam had struggled against the Europeans, and the rule in the Mohammedan world had passed from the Arabs and Persians to the Turks. After the year one thousand, Turkish generals and chieftains had torn the body of Islam, had devastated its land, until at length the heathen Mongols from Central Asia started west against the Turks and in 1258 made the eastern lands of Islam a province of the Mongol empire. Timur the Lame took Bagdad in 1393.

The history of the Nile valley from the time of Saladin to the nineteenth century reads like a phantasmagoria. The promise of high and delicate culture was there; but toward the east rose menacingly the threat of Turkey, forming the right wing of Islam and ready to overwhelm Egypt. If it had not, the history of Europe might have been the history of Egypt. From the west came the steady pressure of a new and virile Negro culture, but one destined to be suddenly arrested by the repulse of the left wing of Islam in Spain, the record of the Sudan, the stubborn resistance of Atlantis overwhelmed by the slave trade to America, and the march of the Bantu toward the Great Lakes.

The effort of this ancient land of Egypt to achieve a new independence and a renewed culture depended on a fusion of Syria and Nubia with Egypt. But the rough and ignorant white slaves, who had lost all culture patterns and learned no new ones, and who nonetheless held all power of government, stifled the budding culture which might have been an African Renaissance and led to futile efforts to conquer Nubia. This distraction of power lost Egypt control of Syria.

Nubia gained independence in 1403, and from the west came the Fung and the people of Darfur, while farther down the Shilluk and Central Africa still resisted. It was in vain that Bibars and Kala'un revived Egypt; most of the fourteenth and fifteenth centuries were filled with struggles of weak and degenerate leaders. Then Selim the Great of the Ottoman empire conquered and annexed Egypt in 1517. Egypt was divided into twenty-four districts, each under Mameluke beys and all under a Turkish pasha. Degeneration set in after the seventeenth century.

Thefts and mutinies filled the sixteenth and seventeenth centuries, and in the eighteenth century the French Revolution tried to unload Napoleon on Egypt and Asia. England thwarted him in far-flung defense of India. In 1811 came Mahemet Alt, a Rumelian, who rid Egypt of the Mameluke beys by deliberate murder and set about the conquest of the Sudan. He overran Nubia in 1820, but lost his son in the mad resistance of the blacks. Meantime he courted Europe by trade and political alliance and tried to share in the profits of the ivory-slave trade. He provoked resistance and rebellion and died a madman in 1849.

His successor, Ishmael, fell into the snare of colonial imperialism, baited by Lord Beaconsfield. Britain saw in the Suez Canal, once conceived by the Pharaohs and dug by the French thousands of years later, a link to unite the British Empire, guard her Indian investment and consolidate her control of trade. Beaconsfield bought the canal from Ishmael after the British and French had involved him hopelessly in debt. When France declined to enter what was to her a doubtful partnership, England practically annexed Egypt to the British Empire.

Why was this? Was it "race"? "Surely," answered the nineteenth century, fattening on the results of Negro slavery and sneering at the mongrels of the Nile valley. But the answer was nothing so simple as the color of a man's skin or the kink of his hair. It was because Egypt during centuries of turmoil and foreign control could achieve no nationhood; because her ancient sources of self-support failed under exploitation, and her ancient culture patterns were submerged and could no longer be renewed from Central Africa by reason of the persistent and continued effort to conquer Nubia. Her new flowering of art in the thirteenth century had died. No democracy could arise in the years from Saladin to Mehemet Ali, and by that time the slave trade for ivory, succeeding the slave trade for sugar, backed by the same demand from Europe and America, had put all Africa beyond the pale of civilization.

One result of Egyptian pressure on Central Africa and its connection with modern colonization is shown by the history of Kilwara in East Africa. The empire was dismembered, the largest share falling to Uganda. When King Mutesa came to the throne of Uganda in 1862, he found Mohammedan influences in his land and was induced to admit Protestants and Catholics. The Protestants, representing British imperialism, tried to convert the king, and the Catholics, representing French imperialism, tried to make him a Catholic. In the midst of this more Mohammedans appeared, seeking also to convert Mutesa. He refused all these faiths and died a rugged pagan.

He was succeeded by his son Mwanga, who distrusted the whites. He ordered the eastern frontier closed against Europeans, and when the Protestant Bishop Hannington attempted to cross in 1885, he had him killed. The Protestants organized against Mwanga, and he banished both Protestants and Catholics. The Mohammedans became the power behind the throne. The Protestants withdrew from Buganda into Angola and organized a united front of Christians against Mohammedans and Mwanga. They captured Mwanga's capital and divided it between Protestants and Catholics. The Mohammedans began to fight back, and finally the Protestants appealed to the British East Africa Company. In 1889 the company dispatched a military mission to Uganda which was later joined by Lugard. Open civil war ensued between Catholics and Protestants.

"At the head of a considerable military force, Captain Lugard of the Imperial British East Africa Company (Ibea), penetrated as far as Mengo, the residence of King Mwanga, and forced upon him a treaty of protectorate; then, turning against the Catholics, he attacked them on some futile pretext, and drove them onto a big island in Lake Victoria. There, around the king and the French missionaries, had gathered a considerable multitude of men, women, and children. Against this helpless and defenseless population Captain Lugard turned his guns and maxims. He exterminated a large number and then, continuing his work of destruction, he gave full rein to his troops and adherents, who burnt all the villages and stations of the White Fathers, their churches and their crops.[22] The British Protestant version of this story varies from this in many particulars.

Mwanga was finally defeated in 1899, taken prisoner and deported. Uganda then became a British protectorate.

So for a thousand years Asia and Africa strove together, renewing their spirits and mutually fertilizing their cultures from time to time, in West Asia, North Africa, the Nile valley, and the East Coast. But at last Europe encompassed them both. In Africa she came to the south as settlers, to the west as slave traders, and to the east as colonial imperialists. Africa slept in a bloody nightmare.

Notes

1. Charles Taüber, *Seafarers and Hieroglyphs* (American Documentation Institute, Washington, D.C.).

2. Rogers, *op. cit.*, Vol. I, p 62.

3. *Ibid.* p. 63.

4. G. Massey, *A Book of the Beginnings* (London: Williams & Norgate, 1881). Vol. I, pp. 18, 218.

5. Edward G. Balfour, ed., "Negro Races," *Cyclopaedia of India* (London: Quaritch, 1885). 3rd ed. Vol. II, p. 1073.

6. Joseph P. Widney, *Race Life of the Aryan Peoples* (New York: Funk and Wagnalls, 1907), Vol. II, pp. 238–39.

7. Quoted in Rogers, *op. cit.*, Vol I, p. 67.

8. Munro, *Prehistoric Japan* (Yokohama: 1911), pp. 676–78.

9. Marcel A. Dieulafoy, *L'Acropole de Suse* (Paris: Hachette et Cie, 1893), pp. 27, 44, 46, 57–86, 102, 115.

10. Harry H. Johnston, *The Negro in the New World*, pp. 24–27.

11. Arnold J. Toynbee, *A Study of History* (London: 1934), Vol. I, p. 226.

12. A letter to J. A. Rogers, December 15, 1922, quoted in Rogers, *op. cit.*, Vol. I, p. 286.

13. *See* Du Bois, *Black Folk*, pp. 41–53.

14. E. Stanley Lane-Poole, *History of Egypt in Medieval Times*, edited by W. M. Flinders Petrie (London: Methuen & Co., 1914), Vol. VI, pp. 22, 28, 89.

15. *Cf.*, *ibid.*, p. 28.

16. *Cf.*, *ibid.*, p. 89.

17. *The Book of Duarte Barbosa*, tr. from the Portuguese by M. L. Davis (London: Hakluyt Society, 1918), Vol. I, pp. 11–13, 18–20.

18. *Memoirs of the History of France* (London: Colburn, 1823–24), 2 nd ed., Vol. III, pp. 152–54, 259–76.

19. W. G. Palgrave, *Narrative of a Year's Journey Through Central and Eastern Arabia* (London: 1866), Vol. I.

20. Ibn Batuta, *Travels in Asia and Africa, 1325–1354*, tr. by H. A. R. Gibb (London: G. Routledge & Sons, 1929), pp. 53, 54, 321, 322, 328, 329, 330.

21. Reginald Coupland, *East Africa and Its Invaders* (Oxford: Clarendon Press, 1938), pp. 32–33.

22. Leonard Woolf, *Empire and Commerce in Africa* (London: Allen and Unwin, n.d.), p. 288.

The Color Line
Belts the World

We have a way in America of wanting to be "rid" of Problems. It is not so much a desire to reach the best and largest solution as it is to clean the board and start a new game. For instance, most Americans are simply tired and impatient over our most sinister social problem, the Negro. They do not want to solve it, they do not want to understand it, they want simply to be done with it and hear the last of it. Of all possible attitudes this is the most dangerous, because it fails to realize the most significant fact of the opening century, viz.: The Negro problem in America is but a local phase of a world problem. "The problem of the twentieth century is the problem of the Color Line." Many smile incredulously at such a proposition, but let us see.

The tendency of the great nations of the day is territorial, political, and economic expansion, but in every case this has brought them in contact with darker peoples, so that we have to-day England, France, Holland, Belgium, Italy, Portugal, and the United States in close contact with brown and black peoples, and Russia and Austria in contact with the yellow. The older idea was that the whites would eventually displace the native races and inherit their lands, but this idea has been rudely shaken in the increase of American Negroes, the experience of the English in Africa, India and the West Indies, and the development of South America. The policy of expansion, then, simply means world problems of the Color Line. The color question enters into European imperial politics and floods our continent from Alaska to Patagonia.

This is not all. Since 732, when Charles Martel beat back the Saracens at Tours, the white races have had the hegemony of civilization—so far as that "white" and "civilized" have become synonymous in every-day speech; and men have forgotten where civilization started.

For the first time in a thousand years a great white nation has measured arms with a colored nation and has been found wanting. The Russo-Japanese war has marked an epoch. The magic of the word "white" is already broken, and the Color Line in civilization has been crossed in modern times as it was in the great past. The awakening of the yellow races is certain. That the awakening of the brown and black races will follow in time, no unprejudiced student of history can doubt.

Shall the awakening of these sleepy millions be in accordance with, and aided by, the great ideals of white civilization, or in spite of them and against them? This is the problem of the Color Line. Force and Fear have hitherto marked the white attitude toward darker races; shall this continue or be replaced by Freedom and Friendship?

The World Problem
of the Color Line

The average American is apt to regard the Negro problem as parochial and temporary: parochial as being largely localized in the Southern United States and temporary as being a passing phase of the slavery problem. On this account he is rather impatient with it. He does not want to discuss or take action because he thinks it but to "leave it to the South" or because he likes to insist that the problem of slavery is closed chapter.

If such men would look carefully around them however they would see that the Problem of the Color Line in America instead of being the closing chapter of past history is the opening page of a new era. All over the world the diversified races of the world are coming into close and closer contact as ever before.

We are nearer China today than we were to San Francisco yesterday.

In this widespread contact of men the problem of humanity is taking new forms and democracy is getting new meanings. The provincial off hand way of settling these matters was to talk of "superior" and "inferior" races, of "lesser breeds without the law." It has been suggested more than once that Christianity was not to apply in these human relations and that the world must revert to the ethics of the club and claw in a great coming war of Races.

In this way many men interpreted the race problem of Negroes and whites in the United States and the West Indies, the contact of Spaniard, Indian, Negro, and Saxon in South America, the looming race disturbances all over Africa, the wide-spread unrest in India and the so-called "Yellow Peril" of China and Japan, not to mention the islands of sea.

If this is true, God help civilization for the struggle will be fierce and disheartening the world over. But it is not true. There is not earthly reason which the ethics of Jesus Christ should not apply to race problems and why we should not use reason in these race problems.

If this is so we should begin right here at home. We should recognize the growing and artificially encouraged race prejudice and we should fight it by all civilized methods. We should insist on civilized treatment for civilized men the world over and human sympathy for all human beings.

The Negro and Imperialism

The government of the United Nations according to the proposals made at Dumbarton Oaks will consist of five great powers comprising perhaps five hundred million white and yellow people who will rule the world through a Security Council and have military power to enforce their decision. However, the three hundred and fifty million yellow people represented by China may not for historic reasons be recognized as racial equals and because of present economic disruption may be largely in the power of white nations. The proposal for a racial-equality declaration among nations, once made by Japan before the League of Nations and lately as persistent rumor has it, repeated at Dumbarton Oaks by China, does not appear in the published proposals.

An indeterminate number of free nations, mostly white folk and comprising about one thousand million people, will function in an assembly in which each nation is represented; the Assembly will have the right of petition, discussion, advice; and action insofar as the Security Council allows. Some of these nations, however, are so under the economic domination of great powers that they will hardly be able to take an independent stand. The Assembly will choose representatives of six nations who will be associated with the great powers in the Security Council; but their ability to influence those powers will depend largely upon the method of voting in the Security Council, which has not yet been decided.

There will be six hundred million colored and black folk inhabiting colonies owned by white nations, who will have no rights that white people are bound to respect. Any revolt on their part can be put down by military force at the disposal of the Security Council. This mass of people will have no right of appeal to the Security Council or to the Assembly.

The Economic and Social Council of the Assembly may make recommendations and consider complaints; but they will apparently have no direct power of investigation; and on this Economic and Social Council no colony will have representation. It may be said that the interests of these colonial peoples will be represented in the world government by the master nations. In the same way it was said in 1787 in the United States that slaves would be represented by their masters.

There is no designated function for the enemy states which have been guilty of imperial aggression in this war. They will comprise perhaps one hundred fifty million people. Presumably they will eventually take their places among the friendly nations and possibly at some day among the great powers.

Evidently the weak point in this outline for a government of men is the fact that at least one-fourth of the inhabitants of the world have no part in it; no democratic power, not even a recognized right of petition. This puts all effort at reform and uplift on the shoulders of imperial countries and does this at a time when the countries, because of loss and disruption in this war, are least able to undertake philanthropic enterprise.

Classifying autonomous colonies like Canada and Australia as Free Nations in the meaning of the proposals, there remain therefore not less than six hundred million persons disfranchised in the General Assembly and represented only by the master nations. In addition there are on earth, a number of other nations, nominally independent, who by reason of accumulated debt owed creditor nations and current control of their labor and industry by absentee capital, will be in no position to act independently or speak freely, even if admitted to seats in the Assembly. Thus perhaps a thousand millions of human beings will have no direct voice, nor exercise any real degree of democratic control in the proposed United Nations.

There is no need here to discuss the advantages or disadvantages of modern imperialism, nor to attempt to assess the gain or loss to peoples arising from their subordination to the great nations. That the colonial system has involved in the past much that was horrible and inhuman will be admitted. That vast numbers of backward peoples have made notable cultural advance under the colonial regime is equally true. Despite this, if the world believes in democracy and is fighting a war of incredible cost to establish democracy as a way of life, it is both intolerable in ethics and dangerous in statecraft to allow, for instance, eight million Belgians to represent ten million Congolese in the new internation [al organization] without giving these black folk any voice even to complain.

It is equally unfair that seven and a half million Portuguese should dominate eleven million in their colonies; or that nine million Dutchmen should be the sole arbiters and spokesmen for sixty-seven million brown men of the South Seas. It cannot be reconciled with any philosophy of democracy that fifty million white folk of the British Empire should be able to make the destiny of four hundred and fifty million yellow, brown and black people a matter solely of their own internal decision. Or again, inside that same empire, it is astonishing to see among the leading "Free Nations," battling for democracy, the Union of South Africa, where two million white folk, not only in international affairs but openly in their established government, hold eight million black natives in a subordination unequalled elsewhere in the world.

This is not for a moment to deny the technique and elementary schools which Belgium has given black Congo; or the fact that the Netherlands has perhaps the most liberal colonial program of any modern empire; or that Great Britain gave the African freedom and education after the slave trade and slavery. But it is equally true that the advance of colonial peoples has been hesitant and slow, and retarded unnecessarily because of the denial of democratic method to the natives, and because their treatment and government have had, and still have, objects and methods incompatible with their best interests and highest progress. The substantial and permanent advance of a group cannot be allowed to depend on the philanthropy of a master, if the desires and initiative of its members are given no freedom, no democratic expression; and if, on the other hand, the will of the master is swayed by strong motives of selfish aggrandizement and gain. How often this selfish interest has prevailed in the past is too well known to require reminder. But today the temptation is stronger rather than less; with Holland reeling under murder, theft and destruction, can the world expect unselfish surrender by the present generation of the profit of rich colonies capable of helping restore her losses? Is it likely that Belgium after her crucifixion will be satisfied with less profit from the Congo and greater expenditure for education, health and social service? With Great Britain straining every nerve to satisfy the demands of her own laboring classes, is it likely that she will of her own initiative extend these reforms to India coupled with the autonomy necessary for Indian initiative and self-government?

No. The united effort of world opinion should now be brought earnestly to bear on the nations owning colonies to make them realize that great as the immediate sacrifice may be, it is the only way to peace. To set up now an internation [al organization] with near half mankind disfranchised and socially enslaved is to court disaster. In the past and the recent past we know how the lure of profit from rich, unlettered and helpless countries, has tempted great and civilized nations and plunged them into bloody rivalry. We know what part colonial aggression has played in this present world disaster. We know that capital investment can earn more in Africa, Asia and the South Seas, because there it suffers few of the restrictions of civilized life; that the foreign investor in these lands is himself the prime ruler and seat of power and without local democratic control, he has but to appease public opinion at home, which is not only ignorant of the local facts, but perhaps all too willing to remain ignorant as long as dividends continue.

If this situation is not frankly faced and steps toward remedy attempted, we shall seek in vain to find peace and security; we shall leave the door wide open for renewed international rivalry to secure colonies and eventually and inevitably for colonial revolt.

Evidently there is indicated here the necessity of earnest effort to avoid the nondemocratic and race-inferiority philosophy here involved. There should be consultation among colonial peoples and their friends as to just what measures ought to be taken. This consultation should look toward asking for the following successive steps:

One, representation of the colonial peoples alongside the master peoples in the Assembly. Whether such representatives should at first have a right to vote or only the right to complain and petition should be determined by the Assembly.

Two, the organization of a Mandate Commission under the Economic and Social Council with distinct power to investigate complaints and conditions in colonies and make public their findings.

Three, a clear statement of the intentions of each imperial power gradually but definitely to take all measures designed eventually to grant the peoples of the colonies political and economic equality with the peoples of the master nations and eventually either to incorporate them into the polity of the master nations or to allow them to become independent free peoples.

We are in this war even more than in the last war facing the problem of democracy: how far are we going to have a world [in which] the people who are ruled are going to have effective voice in their government. We have stated and reiterated that this democratic method of government is going to be applied just as widely as possible. But of course in this program we recognize that beyond the logic of democracy looms the inevitable logic of facts; and the fact is that most of the people of the world have not been ruled in the past by democratic methods; and that the progress toward democracy has been disappointingly slow.

A century ago the explanation of this was clear. You had in the world a minority of people who were capable of civilization; who by their inherent gifts and by long and difficult trial and experience were the natural rulers of the world. They composed most of the white people of the world, although even among those people there was a certain proportion of the lower classes who were incapable because of deficiency in natural gifts to take effective part in democracy.

On the other hand, the majority of the people of the world, composing mainly the colored and black races were naturally so inferior that it was not to be hoped that in any reasonable time, if ever, they would be capable of self-government. This was supposed to be proven by their history, and current scientific investigation seemed to back up historical judgment.

Since the beginning of the twentieth century there has come great change in these judgments. In the first place we have practically given up the idea that there is any considerable portion of the civilized peoples who cannot by education and by the training of experience be made into effective voters and administrators in democratic governments. Further than this we are not nearly so sure today as we used to be of the inherent inferiority of the majority of the people of the earth who happen to be colored. We know, of course, that skin color itself has no particular significance and the other physical characteristics, whatever their significance, are not certain indications of inferiority. [In] the testimony of history we, of course, emphasize the accomplishments of certain people and decry or omit the work of other people. It is always astonishing for Americans to contrast the history of the Revolutionary War as set down in English and American textbooks. In addition to that the testimony of biology and anthropology and of various social sciences convinces us more and more that absolute and essential difference between races as self-perpetuating groups are difficult to fix if not nonexistent. That consequently we have no way of being certain that education and experience will not do for the backward races of man what it has already begun to do for the depressed classes in civilized states.

But these facts do not affect our actions today, because government and economic organization has already built a tremendous structure upon the nineteenth-century conception of race inferiority. This is what the imperialism of our day means. In order, therefore, to judge our present attitude and proposed action toward colonies we must note the growth of the colonial idea.

Roman imperialism did not involve national inferiority. It was simply a matter of political control and centralized taxation with a large degree of autonomy left to the individual states which submitted to Rome. The taxation, to be sure, was often oppressive and amounted to considerable subjection but the Roman Empire was not by any means the counterpart of modern empires. When during the Middle Ages Rome fell to pieces, the world established itself on the basis of separate states who were brought into correspondence with each other through trade and conference. A Marco Polo interpreted an independent Asia to an unknown Europe, and Othello, real or fictitious, was a respected stranger from Africa who offered aid to a European ruler. There arose in Asia and in the Sudan independent kingdoms equal in many respects and certainly distinguished from each other by no evident superiority or inferiority. It was the discovery of America and the sudden demand of labor supplied by the African slave trade that changed this; that based the new European capitalism upon extreme subjection of labor to an organized plantation system; and that rationalized slavery by a new doctrine of inevitable and unchangeable inferiority especially so far as the blacks were concerned.

Negro slavery in America was the passing phase of a great world labor problem but on it was built a new imperialism. Great Britain, from an empire supported by slavery, came to be an empire ruling a wide stretch of countries where cheap labor, more or less compulsory, exported valuable raw material in large quantity to manufacturing centers in the United Kingdom. Other countries followed suit, especially Holland and France. Spain sought to reorganize her empire of conquest and extortion but became in the long run subject to the British organization of industry. Finally Germany and Italy, seeing the tremendous advantage which imperial capital gave to Great Britain, Holland and France, tried to enter into effective competition.

The temptation in this situation was that colonial proprietorship gave the leading countries of the world certain tremendous advantages. The colonial contribution to imperial government was in itself small and often an actual loss; but to the individual investors in these countries, cheap labor and cheap raw material were the basis of tremendous and increasing wealth which made the luxury and power of the late nineteenth and early twentieth centuries remarkable. To enter into rivalry with these countries it was necessary for Germany, Italy and Japan to seek the control of colonies and in that way to gain a vast number of men, wide stretches of land and abundance of raw material.

The First World War was a war of rivalry between imperial powers, with the exploitation of Asia and Africa as the prize to be won. Germany felt that her share in Africa was too small to be commensurate with her manufacturing, commercial and technical possibilities. Japan felt that European imperialism was monopolizing the exploitation of Asia in which she was by situation and race the natural leader.

In the organization of the League of Nations, advantage was taken of the situation of the German colonies to attempt a solution to the whole colonial problem. The German colonies were distributed among France, Great Britain and Japan under the control of a Mandates Commission. The Mandates Commission was supposed to see that the people of these colonies were fairly treated; and that something was done for their social uplift and their economic betterment. The statute that governed the Mandates Commission was, however, deliberately limited in such a way that the Commission really had very little power. It could not of its own initiative inquire into or investigate facts in the various colonies; the colonial peoples themselves had no vested right of appeal to the Commission and as a matter of fact the mandated colony soon became indistinguishable from the other colonies of the countries holding the mandates. It had been hoped that the opposite would happen and that the authority of the Mandates Commission would eventually extend, not only to the former German colonies, but to all colonies of all nations. This never took place and the only organ of the League of Nations that helped the colonial situation was the International Labor Office which succeeded in setting up certain minimum standards of labor usage.

Meantime, between the two world wars there was at first an intensified effort, particularly in the British Empire and to some extent in France, to increase colonial exploitation in order to repay cost of war. This led to bitter complaints especially in British West Africa and finally to a colonial movement there which secured for five of the colonies the right of elected representation in the Governor's Councils; but these councils continued to have a majority of appointed officials representing the home government and also representing large investment interests in England. Elsewhere on the continent, in Kenya and in the Union of South Africa the deprivation of colonial people of their lands continued; while in Asia the new Japanese imperial expansion gained headway and purpose. Among the Dutch colonies some effort was made to increase the participation of colonial peoples in government and to systematize education. In the Belgian Congo elementary education under the Catholic Church was broadened in extent and recognition of local government throughout tribal organizations; but no secondary or high education and no participation in the colonial government was encouraged.

The Second World War, therefore, found the colonial question really unsettled and was precipitated by the determination of Italy to enter upon an imperial career in Africa. On the part of Germany there was a distinct and increasing pressure for the return of her colonies and for even larger colonial expansion. Thus the problem of colonies has been certainly a main cause of two world wars and unless it is frankly faced and its settlement begun, it may easily cause a third.

The colonial organization today is primarily economic. It is a method of carrying on industry and commerce and of distributing wealth. As such it not only confines colonial peoples to a low standard of living and encourages by reason of its high profit to investors a determined and interested belief in the inferiority of certain races but it also affects the situation of the working classes and minorities in civilized countries.

When, for instance, during and after this war the working people of Great Britain, the Netherlands, France and Belgium in particular are going to demand certain costly social improvements from the government: the prevention of unemployment, a rising standard of living, health insurance, increased education of children; the large cost of these improvements must be met by increased public taxation falling with greater weight than ever theretofore upon the rich. This means that the temptations to recoup and balance the financial burden of increased taxation by investment in colonies, where social services are at their lowest and standards of living below the requirements of civilization, are going definitely to increase; and the disposition of parties on the left, liberal parties and philanthropy to press for colonial improvement will be silenced by the bribe of vastly increased help of government to better their condition. The working people of the civilized world will thus largely be induced to put their political power behind imperialism, and democracy in Europe will continue to impede and nullify democracy in Asia and Africa.

In this way the modern world after this war may easily be lulled to sleep and to forget that the exclusion of something between one-fourth and one-half of the whole population of the world from participation in democratic government and socialized wealth is a direct threat to the spread of democracy and a certain promise of future war; and of war not simply as justifiable revolt on the part of colonial peoples who are increasing in intelligence and efficiency, but also of recurring wars of envy and greed because of the present inequitable distribution of colonial gain among civilized nations.

Moreover, the continuation of vested interest in the theory of racial inferiority and the oppression of minorities of any sort will be encouraged by failure to face the problem of the future of colonies.

The American Negro and the Darker World

From the fifteenth through the seventeenth centuries, the Africans imported to America regarded themselves as temporary settlers destined to return eventually to Africa. Their increasing revolts against the slave system which culminated in the eighteenth century, showed a feeling of close kinship to the motherland and even well into the nineteenth century they called their organizations "African," as witness the "African Unions" of New York and Newport, and The African Churches of Philadelphia and New York. In the West Indies and South America there was even closer indication of feelings of kinship with Africa and the East.

The planters' excuse for slavery was advertised as conversion of Africa to Christianity; but soon American slavery appeared based on the huge profits of the "sugar empire" and the "cotton kingdom." As plans were laid for the expansion of the slave system, the slaves themselves sought freedom by increasing revolt which culminated in the eighteenth century. In Haiti they won autonomy; in the United States they fled from the states in the south to the free states in the north and to Canada. Here the Free Negroes helped form the Abolition Movement, and when that seemed to be failing, the Negroes began to plan for migration to Africa, Haiti and South America.

Civil war and emancipation intervened and American Negroes looked forward to becoming free and equal citizens here with no thought of return to Africa or of kinship with the world's darker peoples. However, the rise of the Negro was hindered by disenfranchisement, lynching, and caste legislation. There was some recurrence of the "Back To Africa" idea and increased sympathy for darker folk who suffered the same sort of caste restrictions as American Negroes.

This brought curious dichotomy. In our effort to be recognized as Americans, we American Negroes naturally strove to think American and adopt American folkways. We began to despise all yellow, brown and black peoples. We especially withdrew from all remembrance of kinship with Africa and denied with the white world that Africa ever had a history or indigenous culture. We did not want to be called "Africans" or Negroes and especially not "Negresses." We tried to invent new names for our group. We began to call yellow people "chinks" and "coolies"; and dark whites "dagoes." This was natural under our peculiar situation. But it made us more easily neglect or lose sight of the peculiar change in the world which was linking us with the colored peoples of the world not simply because of the essentially unimportant fact of skin color, but because of the immensely important fact of economic condition.

In the latter part of the eighteenth century, Europe had begun to expand its trade and to import raw materials to be transformed into consumer goods. Machines and methods for manufacture of goods increased tremendously.

When the revolt of the slaves, especially in Haiti, and the moral revolt in England and America, led to the emancipation of slaves, the merchants who had invested in slave labor began to change the form of their investment; they seized colonies in Asia and Africa and instead of exporting native labor used the land and labor on the spot and exported raw materials to Europe for consumption or further manufacture. Immense amounts of wealth for capital were seized by Europeans in India and China, in South America and elsewhere; and thus colonial imperialism arose to dominate the world. Most of the exploited peoples were colored, yellow, brown, and black. A scientific theory arose and was widely accepted which taught that the white people were superior to the colored and had a right to rule the world and use all land and labor for the benefit and comfort of Europeans.

While the emancipation of slaves in America involved great losses for European investors, the simultaneous seizure of wealth in Asia and the new control of colonial labor enabled new rich employers in Europe and North America to accumulate vast sums of capital in private hands and to start the factory system. This method of conducting industry used new inventions and sources of power so as to drive laborers off the land, herd them in factories and reduce them to semi-slavery in Europe, by a wage contract.

This brought the labor movement. In the more advanced European countries labor and its friends fought for more political power, public school education, higher wages and better conditions. These things they gradually secured by union organization and strikes. On the other hand, in Eastern Europe there was little education and wages remained very low. Political power rested in the hands of an aristocracy which became rich through encouraging and protecting western investment. This semi-colonial status of labor was even worse in South and Central America and in the West Indies, while in most of Asia and Africa the condition of colonial labor approached slavery.

Thereupon, arose the doctrine of socialism which demanded that the results of the manufacture of goods and the giving of services go to the labor involved and not mainly to the capitalists. This doctrine was in essence as old as human labor. Primitive labor got all the results of what it did or made. Many early societies like the first Christians and tribes in Africa lived as communal groups, sharing all results of work in common.

Slavery intervened, so that some workers were owned by others; then came aristocracy where a few took the results of the work of the many and the nation became the abode of a rich idle and privileged class who were served by the mass of laborers. Protest against this and the doctrine that income should in some degree become the measure of effort became an increasing demand from the ancient world through the mediaeval world and was studied and scientifically stated by Karl Marx in the first half of the nineteenth century. He proposed that capital belong to the state and that workers run the state. Capitalists vehemently opposed this but were compelled partially to meet the demands of labor by raising wages. In the capitalist nations this raise was more than compensated for by increased profits due to exploitation in colonial and semi-colonial lands. Also, the spread of Democratic control was counterbalanced by hiring white labor to war on colonial labor, and using public taxation for war rather than social purposes.

From the defeat of Napoleon in 1815 to the first world war there was continuous struggle led by white troops armed with the most ingenious weapons to keep colonial peoples from revolt, and most of the peoples of the world in subjection to Western Europe.

This was the situation at the beginning of the twentieth century. British, French, and American capitalists owned the colonies, with the richest natural resources and the best controlled and lowest paid labor. By 1900, they were reaching out for other colonies elsewhere: other nations with fewer or no colonies, led by Germany, demanded a reallotment of colonial wealth. This brought on the First World War.

But, it brought more than this; the assault of Germany and her allies was so fierce that Britain and France had to ask help from their colored colonies. They needed black manpower and without it France would have been overthrown by Germany in the first few months of war. Britain needed food and materials from Asia, Africa, and the West Indies. The United States needed American Negroes who formed an inner labor colony as laborers and stevedores. This meant an increase of wages and rights for colonial peoples. In the United States, it brought the first recognition since 1876 of the equal citizenship of Negroes.

The workers of Eastern Europe, South and Central America were not as badly off as the American serf and Chinese and Indian coolies, but they were sunk in poverty, disease, and ignorance. They were oppressed by their own rich classes working hand in glove with white western investors. When war came they starved and died. The situation became so desperate that Russians and Hungarians refused to fight. Their rulers sought compromise by trying to replace imperial rule with Western European democracy. But the Russian leaders, students of Karl Marx and led by Lenin, demanded a socialist state.

The western world united to forestall this experiment. It said that no socialist state could succeed, but lest it should and lower the profits of capitalists, the effort must be stopped by force of arms. Sixteen capitalist nations, including Britain, France, Germany, the United States, and Japan, invaded Russia and fought for ten years by every means, civilized and uncivilized, to overthrow the plans of the Soviet Union. However, the worldwide collapse of capitalism in 1930, made this attack fail and the world witnessed the founding of the first socialist state.

Then came a new and even more unexpected diversion. The depression which was the partial collapse of capitalism, was so bad in Germany, Spain, and Italy that those states fell into the hands of two dictators, Hitler and Mussolini. Backed by capitalists, they seized power and demanded control not only of the colonial world then dominated by Britain, France, and North America, but domination of the whole world. The west tried to compromise, and offered practically everything demanded, but Hitler's greed and German ambition grew by what they fed upon. They were so convinced of their superior power over the west that Hitler started a Second World War; like the first aimed at control by part of the white race over resources, land, and labor of the rest of the world, he began a wild career. He killed six million Jews, accusing them of being the main cause of the depression and of being an inferior race. He conquered France, and chased the British off the continent. They huddled on their own small island to make a last stand. But, here Hitler paused. He had a new vision. If instead of wasting his power on a desperate England he turned east and seized the semi-colonial lands of the Soviet Union and the Balkan states, then from this central heartland he could win Asia and Africa and after that turn back to deliver the coup de grâce to Britain and America. Hitler thereupon scrapped his treaty with the Soviets, which they, spurned by the west, had been forced to accept; and to the relief of Britain and the United States, Hitler turned to conquer Russia. Englishmen and Americans said with Truman, "Let them kill as many of each other as possible." So, although Hitler's rear was exposed, the western powers held off attack for a year and when they did attack went to the defense of their African colonies and not to aid the Soviet Union. The west was sure that the Soviets would fall in six weeks and thus rid the world of social-ism and Nazis at one stroke.

The result was astonishing. The Soviet Union, almost unaided, conquered Hitler, saved the Baltic states and the Balkans. Roosevelt, Churchill, and Stalin faced a world in which the Soviet Union, Britain, France and the United States must go forward toward a world in which socialism would grow; not perhaps as complete communistic states like the Soviet Union, but in states like the United States and England where social progress under the New Deal and Labor gov-ernment would advance together along paths leading to the same ultimate goal.

This co-operation American business repudiated when it invented the atom bomb. After Roosevelt died, our capitalists determined to drive communism from the world and push socialism back. This cru-sade failed. India became independent and adopted modified social-ism; China conquered the stool-pigeons whom we paid to stop her revolution and became a communist state. The Soviet Union, instead of failing as we predicted, became one of the foremost nations of the earth, with the best educational system and freedom from church dom-ination and second only to this nation in industry. Also the Soviet Union took a legal stand against the color line and stood ready to oppose colonialism. We tried to re-conquer China during the war in Korea and to help France retain Indo-China. But again we failed. Meantime we formed the greatest military machine on earth and spent and are still spending more money preparing for war than ever any other nation on earth at any time has spent.

The excuse for our action is that communism is a criminal conspiracy of evil-minded men and that private capitalism is so superior to socialism that we should use every effort to stop its advance. Here we rest today and to sharpen our aim and concentrate our strength, we starve our schools, lessen social service in medicine and housing, curtail our freedom of speech, limit our pursuit of learning, and are no longer free to think or discuss.

Where now does that leave American Negroes? We cannot teach the peoples of Africa or Asia because so many of them are either communistic or progressing toward socialism, while we do not know what socialism is and can study it only with difficulty or danger. After the First World War we Negroes were in advance of many colored peoples. We started in two ways to lead Africans. In the West Indies, Garvey tried to have Negroes share in western exploitation of Africa. White industry stopped him before he could begin. In the United States Negro churches carried on missionary effort and a few Negroes in 1918 tried to get in touch with Africa so as to share thoughts and plans. Four Pan-African Congresses were held in 1919, 1921, 1923, and 1925, which American, African, and West Indian Negroes attended, and a few persons from Asia and South America. They made a series of general demands for political rights and education. The movement met much opposition. However, it encouraged similar congresses which still exist in all parts of Africa and it was the inspiration back of the mandates commission of the League of Nations and the trusteeship council of the United Nations.

After a lapse of twenty years, a fifth Pan-African Congress was held in England in 1945. It was attended by Negro labor leaders from all parts of Africa and from the West Indies and one from the United States. Especially prominent were the delegates from Kenya and from Ghana, the first independent black dominion of the British Commonwealth. The resolutions adopted here had a clear socialist trend, and further Pan-African Congresses were envisioned to be held in Africa.

Whither now do we go? We American Negroes can no longer lead the colored peoples of the world because they far better than we understand what is happening in the world today. But we can try to catch up with them. We can learn about China and India and the vast realm of Indonesia rescued from Holland. We can know of the new ferment in East, West, and South Africa. We can realize by reading, if not in classrooms, how socialism is expanding over the modern world and penetrating the colored world. So far as Africa is concerned we can realize that socialism is part of their past history and will without a shade of doubt play a large part in their future.

Here in our country, we can think, work and vote for the welfare state openly and frankly; for social medicine, publicly supported housing, state ownership of public power and public facilities; curbing the power of private capital and great monopolies and stand ready to meet and cooperate with world socialism as it grows among white and black.

PART II

Darkwater Rising

Japan and the Color of Imperialism

At last Asia is rising again to that great
and fateful moral leadership of the world
which she exhibited so often in the past
in the lives of Buddha, Mohammad and
Jesus Christ, and now again in the life of Gandhi. We of the Western world
have volubly professed that we believed in the cheek-turning ethics of Jesus
Christ, but seldom, very seldom, have we tried it. Today, an attempt to
conduct a great revolution, the object of which is the emancipation of several
hundred millions of human beings, is being carried on by a program of
passive resistance and civil disobedience. This mighty experiment, together
with the effort of Russia to organize work and distribute income according
to some rule of reason, are the greatest events of the modern world. The
black folk of America should look upon the present birth-pains of the Indian
nation with reverence, hope and applause.

—W. E. B. Du Bois, 1930[1]

Between 1917 and 1935 Du Bois began a significant reconsideration of
the relationship of Asia to the plight of both African Americans and
western imperialism. The Bolshevik Revolution of 1917, what Du
Bois later called, with enthusiasm, the Soviet "experiment," altered
Du Bois's conception of political and racial geography. Whiteness and

white nations no longer signified merely western bourgeoisie. The Soviet commitment to national liberation struggle in South Asia offered new hope that British colonialism might be overthrown. India's satyagraha, or home rule, movement also captivated Du Bois during the 1920s. Lala Rai's friendship, the work of Indian nationals in Berlin and the U.S., the subject of his 1928 novel *Dark Princess*, and the anti-apartheid activities of a young Mahatma Gandhi in South Africa confronted Du Bois with the sudden promise of new global liberation movements. Simultaneously, Japan's growing economic and military strength was the most significant new feature of postwar Asia. The country had emerged from the war a potential competitor or alternative to the interimperialist rivalry of European powers which Du Bois understood World War I to be. Even China was stirring after the war: the rise of a Communist Party there presented a new challenge to feudal order and captured Du Bois's attention as still another possible challenge to the long colonial history of Asia.

Du Bois was fairly bursting with enthusiasm about the potential of this new, nascent Pan-Asianism in October of 1936 when he published "The Union of Colour" in *The Aryan Path*, a prominent Indian nationalist journal. The essay was a rejoinder to an essay by Indian pacifist N. S. Subba Rao cautioning nations of color not to divide the world in two by aligning against white (mainly European) supremacy. Du Bois noted that American "Negroes" had frequently heard such go-slow arguments, and denounced this "self denying attitude" as "disastrous": ". . . if the coloured world wants to meet the white world on a plane of real equality and effective brotherhood, and without compromise and doubt evolve and establish a real union of all colours and race," he wrote, "then first of all the coloured world must be a strong world, strong in its own inner organization, strong in its power of thought and defence."

For a good part of the 1930s, Du Bois perceived Japan as the model of this new Asian autonomy. Its "aggression" in China, and the emerging tensions between the two countries in the early 1930s, was a test case, Du Bois thought, of two radically different historical paths open to the colonized countries of the world: militant self-defense, or nation-building, and a kind of flaccid obeisance that fulfilled, tragically, imperialism's prescription. "I do not want to supplement the hegemony of the white race with a tyranny of black folk or yellow folk or brown folk" he wrote. "I want the best of mankind to be able to work together for the development of all men. But I am not going to let my wish blind me into thinking that this object is accomplished if I proceed to give up my manhood and acquiesce spinelessly in continued suppression. That path leads to disaster and leads just as swiftly as the path of threats and braggadocio."

The selections from this section, focusing on Du Bois's journalistic and essayistic writings on Japan and China, serve as a bridge and pivot point in Du Bois's view of Asia's place in the making of the twentieth century. It begins with "The Union of Colour" and is followed by "The Clash of Colour: Indians and American Negroes." The title of the latter, published in *The Aryan Path* on March 7, 1936, serves to lay out the problem of the world color line resolved in "The Union of Colour." The essay circles the internal shadow of the color line—caste prejudice and racial self-hatred—as the twin pillars of colonial abjection. Their creation is informed and exacerbated by the simultaneous neglect and ignorance of racial understanding between blacks and Asians fostered by colonial rule, geographic distance, and the ideology of white supremacy. "European exploitation desires the black slave, the Chinese coolie and the Indian labourer for the same ends and the same purposes, and calls them all 'niggers'" wrote Du Bois. In an effort to explode the binary of what Fanon would call black skin, white masks, Du Bois linked the fate and fortunes of the "labouring masses" of Africa and Asia, a forerunner of his analysis in "The Negro and Imperialism" and "The American Negro and the Darker World."

Prior to his travels to China and Japan, Du Bois demonstrated both optimism and frustration as he perceived the two countries veering towards confrontation. "Japan and Ethiopia," first published in *Crisis* in 1933, anticipates the possibility of an Asian-African alliance formed out of economic collaboration between the two nations—an interesting anticipation of African American support for Ethiopia after its invasion by Italy. Yet in the same year Du Bois chides China and Japan for appearing to be at competitive loggerheads—a worrisome family quarrel to Du Bois that threatened to undermine Asian and colored solidarity. In the essays and journalistic reports that follow, Du Bois uses both firsthand accounts of his travels in China, Japan and Russia in 1936 and 1937 to tease out both the potentialities and pitfalls of a climactic encounter between Asian neighboring states. The reports are fascinating for revealing Du Bois in a relaxed, itinerant, touring mode—he is a travel writer on a political mission to describe the contours of new colored nationhood. Typical to the genre, he at times uses analogy and anecdote as the basis of his understanding, seeking to "map" his experience of displacement onto itself and what he knows from the American and African American world he has left behind. Because they were written as a series of weekly columns in the *Pittsburgh Courier*, the reports demonstrate the evolution and change in Du Bois's analysis of events on the ground in Japan and China especially. In the Spring of 1937, for example, Du Bois is almost unequivocal in his praise for the Japanese occupation of China and Manchuria. The shadow of his own racial romanticism tinges his observation that racism is simply not possible between national groups he perceives in primitive racialist terms as kin. Yet beginning with his report of September 25, 1937, Du Bois redoes the calculus of his earlier reportage. "It is to escape annihilation and subjection and the nameless slavery of Western Europe that Japan has gone into a horrible and bloody carnage with her own cousin," he writes; "but the cause and the blame of the war lies on England, and France, and America; on Germany and Italy; on all those white nations, which for a hundred years and more, have by blood and rapine forced their rule upon colored nations." Du Bois moves on one hand closer to critical condemnation of Japanese expansion, but dialectically deeper into analysis of its historical and material causes. Here, as throughout his career, Asia provided Du Bois important challenges to thinking about the relationship of global totality of capital, on one hand, and the relationship of the world's colored people on the other.

Later, in *The Black Flame, A Trilogy*, Du Bois retold the whole of his 1930s Asian travels through the loose veil of fictional biography. Du Bois's imagined persona, Mansart, in the chapter here entitled "The Color of Asia," serves as a kind of wiser—literally omniscient—version of the earlier traveler. To mark these distinctions, Du Bois mixes excerpted passages from his earlier journalistic accounts of his travels with reflections on what Mansart has come to learn in retrospect about his voyages. In an important passage again on Japan and the causes and consequences of imperialism, Du Bois is more sharply critical and summative than in his newspaper columns. "To me," he writes about the period of the late 1930s to the denouement of Japanese power at the end of World War II, "the tragedy of this epoch was that Japan learned Western ways too soon and too well, and turned from Asia to Europe. She had a fine culture, an exquisite art, and an industrial technique marvelous in workmanship and adaptability . . . . She might have led Asia and the world into a new era. But her headstrong leaders chose to *apply Western imperialism* to her domination of the East, and Western profit-making replaced Eastern idealism" (emphasis mine). Du Bois's formula is a kind of inversion of Orientalist logic. It is the *West's* moral and material corruption which infects and inhabits and corrupts an idealized corpus of Japanese culture. Du Bois's penchant for juxtaposing the refined cultural (Asia) and vulgar economic (West) is his formula for exposing the greedy visible hand of Western empire shown strangling the potential newborn of Asian harmony and world ascent in its crib.

The consequences of this resolution were profound for Du Bois. In "A Chronicle of Race Relations," his regular column platform in

Phylon, the journal of race published at Atlanta University, Du Bois began to survey race and race relations across the globe at a moment, Du Bois sensed, of imminent catastrophe and change. In a 1940 column included here, Du Bois laments that much of Eastern Europe is itself now in the stranglehold of German race supremacy. Meanwhile, India and the rest of Asia, including the territories of Java and Madura in the Dutch East Indies, lay desperate under the hands of colonialism, dying, but fighting back. Du Bois perceives virtually no way out of a encroaching white world domination— except in the person of Mahatma Gandhi. The essay ends with lengthy quotations from the figure Du Bois singled out from the Asian pantheon as his favorite (elsewhere he compared him favorably to Lenin, and during the civil rights era, asserted his importance even over that of Martin Luther King as an influence on nonviolent strategy). Almost wistfully, Du Bois hopes that Gandhi's whispers of "satyagraha" will be heard above the din of German Fascism's strident call. The piece concludes this section because it predicts not only the centrality of India's national liberation struggles for Du Bois's anticolonial politics during the 1940s and 1950s, but because it points to the Second World War as a kind of imperial apocalypse, or endpoint in Du Bois's thought. He was a radical, and radically changed figure after World War II, which crushed his hopes that racial inequality, the inequitable distribution of wealth, interimperialist rivalry, and especially United States power could be challenged by any other means than world revolution. World War II, that is, showed Du Bois that imperialism of any color was a disaster, that nationalism had profound and permanent limitations, and that Asia was bound to be the vanguard site of struggle between Western imperialism and experiments in opposition.

Note

1. "Postscript," *Crisis*. V. 37, n. 7 (1930): p. 246.

Publication History for Part II

"The Union of Colour." *Aryan Path*, V. 7 (October 1936): pp. 483–84.

"The Clash of Colour: Indians and American Negroes." *Aryan Path*, V. 8 (March 1936): pp. III–15.

"Listen Japan and China." *Crisis*, V. 40, n. 1 (1933).

"Japan and Ethiopia." *Crisis*, V. 40, n. 12 (1933).

"Man Power." *Pittsburgh Courier* (March 6, 1937).

"What Japan Has Done." *Pittsburgh Courier* (March 20, 1937).

"The Yellow Sea." *Pittsburgh Courier* (Feb. 20, 1937).

"China and Japan." *Pittsburgh Courier* (Sept. 25, 1937).

"The Color of Asia." In *Worlds of Color: The Black Flame: A Trilogy*. Millwood, NY: Kraus-Thomson Organization, Ltd., pp. 62–70.

"A Chronicle of Race Relations." *Phylon*, V. 1, n. 3 (1940): pp. 270–88.

The Union of Colour

I have read with interest and substantial agreement Mr. N. S. Subba Rao's article in the May number of *The Aryan Path*. With most of it, I am in complete agreement, but there is one paragraph in which lurks, as it seems to me, all of the danger which I tried to point out in my original article. Mr. Subba Rao says:

> In the closing years of the nineteenth century, the success of Japan roused the Kaiser to call upon the nations of Europe through a famous cartoon, to unite themselves against the Yellow Peril, and it is just as easy and unwise to call upon the coloured peoples to league themselves against the white races. Narrow loyalties can be developed, and unholy passions roused, by dwelling on one's disabilities and dangers, which can always be attributed to others. Swift and violent action unhappily appeals to mankind, but if the results are to endure the path towards a new and stable order lies through reason and persuasion. To range the forces of the world into two camps, sullen, suspicious and menacing, is no answer.

We Negroes in the United States have repeatedly passed through this phase of reasoning, We have said: "You must not unite or seem to unite against white people. You must not organize in opposition. You must not even think of yourselves as by any possibility existing apart from them or with an object of your own." The result of this self-denying attitude is easily disastrous. There is no hesitancy on the part of the European peoples in thinking of their own destiny and of their work and future without reference to the rest of the world. And as a result, they go on from strength to strength, and from organization to organization.

If now the Asiatic and African worlds are going to think of themselves only as appendages of the European world; if they are going to refuse to envisage a future quite independent of Europe, if necessary—and even in opposition to well-known European aims—the result is bound to be weakness, defeatism and lack of all organized power. On the other hand, if the coloured world wants to meet the white world on a plane of real equality and effective brotherhood, and without compromise and doubt evolve and establish a real union of all colours and of races, then first of all the coloured world must be a strong world, strong in its own inner organization, strong in its power of thought and defence. Without this there will come to the council table of the world's interests a cringing beggar instead of an upstanding man.

I know, of course, the implications of all this. It will be said, as Mr. Subba Rao hints: That this means war and struggle and the prolonging of that awful path of blood through which humanity has staggered thus far. I realize all that, but I maintain on the other hand, that unless the coloured peoples are strong and prepared, the path of humiliation and degradation, of insult and suppression, which they will inevitably continue to tread will be much more disastrous to the world's future than anything else could possibly be.

It is too true that only two awful paths seem to face the suppressed peoples of to-day: The path of humiliation, and the path of war. What I am afraid of is that the coloured peoples are going to discount the terrible effects of continued and insistent humiliation. It is impossible to bring up self-reliant manhood if the children of India, Africa and Negro America are going to be brought up under the incubus of colour caste; and what I propose is a hearty and even a desperate attempt to find *a third path*—a path that will not necessarily range the forces of the world into "two camps, sullen, suspicious and menacing," but which will aim at inner cohesion and understanding among the coloured peoples, and especially organization designed to meet and solve their pressing economic problems.

I believe that by consumers' co-operation and production, a thoughtful and scientific blending of the preachments of Gandhi and Kagawa, we can stop the dependence of coloured consumers upon white exploitation; that we can establish new ideals of mutual respect which shall not be exclusively and continually white ideals.

I cannot see that this path must necessarily lead to war unless the white world openly and flatly insists that any organization of coloured folk for the advance of coloured folk is a menace to white people; and in that case, a war of races and of colours is absolutely inevitable; and not inevitable because I and others have raised the flag of warning, but simply because of the impossible attitude of the European and American world. On the other hand, it is just as possible that when through inner organization and developed strength the coloured worlds grow in power and efficiency, they will strengthen the liberal thought of the white world; help to abolish war and armament, and make all reasonable men among the white nations come to their senses, and come to their senses all the more quickly when they see the inevitable cost of policy of forcible suppression.

I believe in man; in men of all colours and races. I do not want to supplement the hegemony of the white race with a tyranny of black folk or yellow folk or brown folk. I want the best of mankind to be able to work together for the development of all men. But I am not going to let my wish blind me into thinking that this object is accomplished if I proceed to give up my manhood and acquiesce spinelessly in continued suppression. That path leads to disaster and leads just as swiftly as the path of threats and braggadocio.

The Clash of Colour

Indians and American Negroes

The great difficulty of bringing about understanding, sympathy and co-operation between the Negroes of America and the peoples of India lies in the almost utter lack of knowledge which these two groups of people have of each other.

First of all, the Negroes, taught in American schools and reading books and articles by American writers, have almost no conception of the history of India. It practically has no place in our curriculum and references to that great past which every Indian knows bring no intelligent comprehension on the part of the Negroes in America.

On the other hand, the knowledge which educated Indians have of the American Negro is chiefly confined to the conventional story spread by most white American and English writers: ignorant black savages were enslaved and made to do physical labour which was the only thing they could do. They were finally emancipated by a benevolent government and given every aid to rise and develop. Much of this aid was mistaken, as, for instance, the bestowing of the right to vote, and proved a hindrance rather than a help. To-day these Negroes are contented labourers occupying that lower sphere for which they are especially adapted.

This false knowledge and lack of knowledge in the two groups are now emphasized by the modern methods of gathering and distributing news. To the editors of the great news agencies, Indians and Negroes are not news. They distribute, therefore, and emphasize only such things as are bizarre and uncommon: lynchings and mobs in the Southern States of the United States, dialect and funny stories; and from India, stories of religious frenzy, fights between Hindus and Mohammedans, the deeds of masters of magic and the wealth of Indian princes.

To this is added deliberate and purposeful propaganda, so that from American newspapers Negroes get no idea of the great struggle for freedom and self-government which has been going on in India, or of that deep philosophy of the meaning and end of human life which characterizes the Indian nation. They only hear of what England has done to develop India and to keep the peace.

On the other hand, few Indians know of Negroes able to do more than read and write, of the Negro literature that has been growing and expanding for seventy-five years, and of the leaders who have done their part, not only in the development of black men, but in the development of white America.

To all this must be added the almost insuperable bars of religious difference. Negroes have long been enmeshed in a veil of sectarian Christianity which regards all peoples as "Heathen" who are not Christian, and all Christians as suspect who are not Protestants, and no Protestant as a candidate for Heaven unless he believes in the Trinity and the "Plan of Salvation."

The Indian, also, finds it difficult to conceive of intelligent men who have no real knowledge of either Buddha or Mohammed, and no religious philosophy that forms a part of their real life.

Much of this lack of knowledge and misapprehension might be avoided if Indians and Negroes had a chance to meet and know each other; but they are at opposite ends of the earth and, so far as American Negroes are concerned, deliberate and other difficulties are put in the way of their meeting. It is difficult for an American Negro to get the English Government to *vise* his passport for a visit to India and if the *vise* is obtained, usually it is under pledge to limit his words and activities. The accommodations offered by steamships often involve racial discrimination, while the cost of such trips is of course prohibitive to the mass of Indians and Negroes.

On the other hand, a number of Indians visit America; but unless they are as wise and catholic as my friend, the late Lajpat Rai, they are apt to see little and know less of the twelve million Negroes in America. First of all, they meet a peculiar variation of the Colour Line. An Indian may be dark in colour, but if he dons his turban and travels in the South, he does not have to be subjected to the separate-car laws and other discriminations against Negroes in that part of the country where the mass of Negroes live. This public recognition of the fact that he is not a Negro may, and often does, flatter his vanity so that he rather rejoices that in this country at least he is not as other dark men are, but is classified with the Whites.

This, however, applies primarily to the Indian with money enough to travel and live in comfort. If he should try for employment or for citizenship or any economic status, he would find the tables quite turned, and that, while an African Negro can become a citizen of the United States, an Indian of the highest caste cannot.

All this is of course but the foolishness and illogic of race discrimination and most intelligent Indians would only need to be reminded of it to insist upon opportunity to see and know American Negroes. This was certainly the case of Rabindranath Tagore and many other prominent Indians who have visited America.

Indian visitors must, of course, remember that they will have to make some special effort to see the Negro world. It is a world largely apart and organized; in its churches, industry and amusement, largely separate from the white world. It is not easily penetrated by strangers, except in lines of commercialized entertainment. The Harlem cabarets do not, for instance, represent Negro life, but are simply commercialized investments of white men with Negro music and entertainment.

On the other hand, for visitors who wish to know Negroes and try to carry out their wish, no great difficulties are encountered. The Negro churches always welcome visitors, and Negro organizations are glad to give them opportunity to speak and to ask questions, and even Negro homes are open to sympathetic strangers.

In the North, such intercourse is easy and normal. In the South, it is more difficult; and in the South some eight million of the twelve million of the American Negroes live. But even there, through the universities and colleges and the private and public schools, through churches and homes, necessary contacts may be made.

The percentage of visitors between these groups must always be small, but a vast amount of work can be done through literature and especially literature directed toward the masses of these two peoples. The best effort in this line is Lajpat Rai's *United States*; he seeks not simply to write a conventional history of white America for the information of coloured India, but gives a quarter of his space and intelligent interpretation to the Negro problem in the United States. He could do this because, during his enforced exile from his native land, he gained wide acquaintance with American Negroes and travelled over much of the United States. It is unfortunate that American Negroes have not made a similar study of India to orientate the thought of the people concerning the problems of that land.

There are in the United States one hundred or more weekly newspapers circulating among Negroes, of which eight or ten have considerable circulation. It would be an excellent thing if contributions from India, explaining the history and problems of the land, should appear in these papers; and on the other hand, the press of India ought to welcome a number of Negro contributors with explanations of their situation here.

Despite the difficulties, there must be greater conscious effort to get these groups into sympathetic understanding. Indians appeared in the four or five Pan-African Congresses which were held and which were of course only tentative efforts toward a greater ideal. In the future, congresses including Indians and Negroes ought to meet periodically, not necessarily for action, but for understanding, and especially for emphasizing the fact that these people have common aims.

It is this fact, or the failure to recognize it, which causes the lack of knowledge and understanding between these groups. To most

Indians, the problem of American Negroes—of twelve million people swallowed in a great nation, as compared with the more than three-hundred millions of India—may seem unimportant. It would be very easy for intelligent Indians to succumb to the widespread propaganda that these Negroes have neither the brains nor ability to take a decisive part in the modern world. On the other hand, American Negroes have long considered that their destiny lay with the American people; that their object was to become full American citizens and eventually lose themselves in the nation by continued intermingling of blood. But there are many things that have happened and are happening in the modern world to show that both these lines of thought are erroneous. The American Negroes belong to a group which went through the fire of American slavery and is now a part of the vast American industrial organization; nevertheless it exists as representative of two hundred or more million Negroes in Africa, the West Indies and South America. In many respects, although not in all, this group may be regarded as the leading intelligentsia of the black race and no matter what its destiny in America, its problems will never be settled until the problem of the relation of the white and coloured races is settled throughout the world.

India has also had temptation to stand apart from the darker peoples and seek her affinities among whites. She has long wished to regard herself as "Aryan" rather than "coloured" and to think of herself as much nearer physically and spiritually to Germany and England than to Africa, China or the South Seas. And yet the history of the modern world shows the futility of this thought. European exploitation desires the black slave, the Chinese coolie and the Indian labourer for the same ends and the same purposes, and calls them all "niggers."

If India has her castes, American Negroes have in their own internal colour lines the plain shadow of a caste system. For American Negroes have a large infiltration of white blood and the tendency to measure worth by the degree of this mulatto strain.

The problem of the Negroes thus remains a part of the world-wide clash of colour. So, too, the problem of the Indians can never be simply a problem of autonomy in the British commonwealth of nations. They must always stand as representatives of the coloured races—of the yellow and black peoples as well as the brown—of the majority of mankind, and together with the Negroes they must face the insistent problem of the assumption of the white peoples of Europe that they have a right to dominate the world and especially so to organize it politically and industrially as to make most men their slaves and servants. This attitude on the part of the white world has doubtless softened since the World War. Nevertheless, the present desperate attempt of Italy in Ethiopia and the real reasons back of the unexpected opposition on the part of the League of Nations show that the ideals of the white world have not yet essentially changed. If now the coloured peoples—Negroes, Indians, Chinese and Japanese—are going successfully to oppose these assumptions of white Europe, they have got to be sure of their own attitude toward their labouring masses. Otherwise they will substitute for the exploitation of coloured by white races, an exploitation of coloured races by coloured men. If, however, they can follow the newer ideals which look upon human labour as the only real and final repository of political power, and conceive that the freeing of the human spirit and real liberty of life will only come when industrial exploitation has ceased and the struggle to live is not confined to a mad fight for food, clothes and shelter; then and only then, can the union of the darker races bring a new and beautiful world, not simply for themselves, but for all men.

Listen, Japan and China

Colossi of Asia and leaders of all colored mankind: for God's sake stop fighting and get together. Compose your quarrels on any reasonable basis. Unite in self-defense and assume that leadership of distracted mankind to which your four hundred millions of people entitle you.

Listen to a word from twelve little black millions who live in the midst of western culture and know it: the intervention of the League of Nations bodes ill for you and all colored folk. There are philanthropists and reformers in Europe and American genuinely interested in all mankind. But they do not rule, neither in England nor France, not in Germany nor in America. The real rulers of the world today, who stand back of Stimson, Macdonald and Herriot, are blood-sucking, imperial tyrants who see only one thing in the quarrel of China and Japan and that is a chance to crush and exploit both. Nothing has given them more ghoulish glee than the blood and smoke of Shanghai and Manchuria or led them to rug hands with more solemn unction and practised hypocrisy.

Unmask them, Asia; tear apart their double faces and double tongues and unite in peace. Remember Japan, that white America despises and fears you. Remember China, that England covets your land and labor. Unite! Beckon to the three hundred million Indians; drive Europe out of Asia and let her get her own raped and distracted house in order. Let the yellow and brown race, nine hundred million strong take their rightful leadership of mankind. Let the young Chinese and Japanese students and merchants of America and Europe cease debate and recrimination while gleeful whites egg them on. Get together and wire word to Asia. Get together China and Japan, cease quarrelling and fighting! Arise and lead! The world needs Asia.

Japan and Ethiopia

It is reported, upon how good authority we do now know, that Japan and Ethiopia have entered into an economic treaty by which Japan is to receive 16,000,000 acres for Japanese colonization and Ethiopia is to be repaid by Japanese ingenuity, trade and friendship. If this is true, we shall be extremely pleased. It would be a rapprochement between Asia and Africa which foreshadows closer union between yellow and black people. We have no illusions about the Japanese motives in this matter. They are going to Ethiopia for purposes of profit. At the same time the treatment of Ethiopia by England and Italy and France has been so selfish and outrageous that nothing Japan can do can possibly be worse. America has only been in the background because of her distance and her fear that her own black population might get interested. When once there is unification and reasonable oneness of purpose between Japan and China, and then between these two great nations and India, and finally between yellow Asia and black Africa, a new era will open in the world and the impossible domination of one mad race will end.

Man Power

Three things attract white Europe to China: cheap women; cheap child-labor; cheap men. And these same three things, too, attract and build the power of Chinese and Japanese capitalists. Everywhere one sees men doing what machines do in Europe and America: pile-driving, pumping water, acting like beasts of burden, crowding in great masses begging to delve and dig and carry for a pittance. Labor is cheap— dirt cheap—and yet the Chinese babies pour into the world. It is fantastic.

There are forces and counter-acting efforts. The Koumingtang is a government of one part like Communism in Russia, Hitlerism in Germany and Fascism in Italy. But it has peculiar difficulties in Chinese conditions: the immensity of the land and population; the break-down of all central government for a long series of years, and cata-strophes; the retreat of social control to the curious Chinese family unit, perhaps the strongest single social unit in the world today. Entrenched here in almost impenetrable walls of custom, religion and industry, the attempts at reform meet a rock wall of opposition and misunderstanding. The new young China has attacked the problem bravely, even slowly and by piecemeal; and then comes the shadow of war to dissipate nearly all their energies. War with bandits, war with Russia, war with Japan; all threaten or are real at times. The problem of China is perhaps more intricate than the problem of the races of Africa in America and Africa. But there is a mighty heritage of culture never ruined that still exists to help China. But China turns to war. Everywhere are soldiers. School girls where I visit are making silk bulletproof jackets for the soldiers putting down revolt in Mongolia. Bandits must be driven from the teeming interior provinces. European alliances must be watched; and always Japan. Curiously enough, when China speaks of the "last war" she does not mean the World War, but the struggle with Japan in 1932.

The Chinese City

The Chinese City again and again leaps to attention. Like the Chinese, it is unique. It is a series of satisfactions; not merely for the few, for the rich, for the well-to-do, but for everybody. It has color—flamboyant color of banners, streamers, flags, lanterns. It has sound—not only a babel of human voices, but cries of selling, song and now the shrieking radio. It has a companionship for everybody, no one lonesome, no one, or at least not every one, exclusive. There is food and drink, inconceivably cheap, perhaps dirty, but hot and abundant, and cooked exactly to the customer's liking. There is fortune-telling, sober silent rows of seers and paraphernalia, not mocking and cynical, but earnest. There is gambling, but usually games of chance or skill, not rigged cheating. Skills are for sale carving, fashioning, making: there are services of barber, and hairdresser. There is systematic begging and sale of all imaginable. There is shelter and the promise of cure for ill and healing. The Chinese city fascinates and holds millions. It is cheap life for a poor people, whom it satisfies.

What Japan Has Done

The accomplishment of Japan has been to realize the meaning of European aggression on the darker peoples, to discover the secret of the white man's power, and then without revolutionary violence is change her whole civilization and attitude toward the world, so as to emerge in the twentieth century the equal in education, technique, health, industry and art of any nation on earth. It was a colossal task. It called for sacrifice of the noblest sort. It called for genius. It called for team work. All this involved cost. It cost freedom and meant severe discipline. It meant severe repression. It meant force. But it was accomplished, and Japan is proud.

But in her very pride and accomplishment lies danger. The Europe which she copied was no perfect land. The technique of industry which Japan mastered, the capitalistic regime which she adopted so successfully has, as all thinking men see today, threatening, if not fatal tendencies; and now with a herculean task just behind her Japan is called again to lead world revolution, and lead it with the minimum of violence and upheaval. In the nineteenth century Japan saved the world from slavery to Europe. In the twentieth century she is called to save the world from the slavery to capital.

Japan's Present Position

Japan today has a tremendous advantage. She owns and controls her own capital. She need beg neither Wall nor Lombard Street for capital.

She has her own engineers and technicians. Above all, she has a labor force that can live in contentment and health at twenty-five cents a day per family. Consequently, she is beating the commercial world today, and underselling every nation in the world markets. She is reaching out with her capital and technique and controlling industry in China and some parts of the South. World commerce is beginning to depend on Japanese goods. Go to any Woolworth store and see. Japanese labor in Japan is displacing white labor in England, France, Germany, and America.

Japan's Danger

Japan today is thinking in terms of capitalistic advance and not primarily in terms of human culture. Her attitude toward China is the main case in point. In the nineteenth century Japan had to protect China against herself, or otherwise Europe from the domination of the Chinese would have sunk little Japan into the sea. Chinese patriots today may not forget that they owe their chance for independence today to the fight of Japan against European aggression. The great war made it impossible for Europe to dominate the East, and the world war was caused by unbridled capitalism. Japan after the war determined to dominate China and other parts of Asia, so as to make a recurrence of European aggression impossible. This is the secret of her military policy. But Japan forgets the danger of capitalism. Unbridled production cannot continue indefinitely. Cheap labor is not in the end cheap for the nation that seeks to build property on it. If Japan today, avoiding temptation, raised the standard of living among her laborers, she could still compete with the world and at the same time develop a mass of workers who would be the most intelligent and gifted the world has ever seen. Democracy would become possible in a great land based on a really intelligent people. Industry would exist not for production, but for the widest and most profitable consumption, made possible by rational distribution of such goods as the people really need for their weal.

England and Japan

It is the fear of England that is pushing Japan in an opposite direction. England dominates China and India, Australia and New Zealand. But for the grace of God and the vigilance of the Japanese, she would own Japan. At one time during and after the Russo-Japanese war, recognizing the power and ability of the Japanese, England made alliance with her as an equal. Then with no reason except the unstated one of color prejudice in America, South Africa and Australia and even Britain, of unwillingness to link her fortune with yellow people, the alliance lapsed in 1931. When after the world war, China was disintegrating, Japan knew that unless she seized Manchuria, Europe would; just as England seized and holds Hong-Kong; France, Annam; and Germany and Russia large and larger slices, before the war. When Japan seized that part of China which was nearest anarchy, England, America and the white world howled, and are still howling. China braced herself and, protected by European weakness and Europe's fear of Japan, began a forward development. But she let her bitterness toward Japanese aggression become a leading motive in her quest for new unity and strength forgetting all about the worse and longer aggressions of white Europe. Japan found herself between the devil and deep blue sea; rapprochement with China, based on blood kinship and cultural likeness, was stopped by war and boycott, that reached unbelievable depths of hatred. Europeans secretly and openly encouraged a split between colored people which played directly into their hands. English papers today in Shanghai detail with calm impartiality every scrap of news and gossip calculated to inflame China against Japan. Then came rearmament in Europe, with Japan outside. There seemed nothing for her to do but seek alliance with

Germany and Italy, despite the fact that Germany despises yellow races, and Italy's hand are red with the blood of Africa.

Japan and Russia

Worst of all, this alliance of Japan with Fascism sets her own as the enemy of Russia. It was, of course, logical for Japan to recoil from her first European antagonist, whose defeat placed her in the family of nations. Moreover, certain points of the Russian revolution touched Japan on the raw—the attack on family and religion. But the Japanese family group was widely different from what Russia rightly attacked, and the Russian Orthodox Church had no remotest resemblance to Shinto cultural traditions and customs, or even to tolerant Buddhism as it exists in Japan. These things disposed Japan to oppose the Soviets. But, of course, the underlying motive was the fear among the capitalists. Japanese industry is controlled by the great groups of capitalists. They are generous and patriotic men. They have been helped and often financed and furnished technique by the government, at the expense of the taxpayer. They would not and could not deny and demand of the government in the line of taxation or co-operation. But they are capitalists, completely subjected to the domination of the private profit motive. They are allied with international capital. They fear communism. Yet their supremacy in government influence is not as great as in many European lands. Above them stands the tradition of Imperial authority, the power of the essentially communistic Japanese family and the deep belief in the Japanese people. There is poverty in Japan; there is oppression; there is still ignorance. But nowhere in the modern world is there such a high literacy, as newspaper circulations of three, and even five million prove; the Japanese laborer is probably the most contented in the world, and this is not the content of stupor, but rather of simple wants and joys.

Where then, in spite of cruel misunderstanding and frustrations; in spite of the rule of wealth and industry for private profit; in spite of the dominant military spirit, no worse but just as bad as in America—where else in the modern world is there a people so intelligent, so disciplined, so clean and punctual, so instinctively conscious of human good and ill, as the Japanese? And where can the world better look for leadership eventually toward industry based on well being and not on private profit, and to a democracy which includes the masses of people and is conducted for their benefit?

Japan is far from this now. Few vote and votes are limited in power. Wealth rules in Tokyo as well as in New York, London and Paris. But what Japan did yesterday, she can do tomorrow.

The Yellow Sea

My last day in Dairen was spent at Port Arthur, and in lecturing. I lectured at 4:30 to about three hundred persons on "Race Segregation," touching the Negro, Japanese, Chinese, Mexican and southeast European problems. I spoke in English and an interpreter translated. At seven we had a round table and very frank and informing conference. Then in the morning I went down to the great harbor of Dairen. My friend handed me three colored streamers of farewell and, following the beautiful Japanese custom, I and a dozen others held one end while the friends ashore unwound the other ends until a rainbow of colored strips of paper streamed from ship to shore and bade Manchoukuo good-bye.

We sailed into the Yellow Sea on a perfect day. Rough brown mountains lined the left, with oil refineries and factories, boats and trains. Then further out the hills became barren except where the Japanese with infinite patience are covering them with tiny pine trees, whose sturdy roots will some day in fifty years break up the barren waste which Russia left and clothe the hills again in green. Further and further the mountains retreated on our left. A precipitous isle came and went and we were on the open water, sailing to China. I went out to watch the death of day. The sun was a ball of beaten gold, with pink and purple cloud streamers floating east. Quickly it became a flattened burning egg resting on the horizon. Then it fell into the green waters of the Yellow Sea, hissing with silent light, and sending glory cries to high heaven.

China

China is inconceivable. I have been here four days, and I am literally dazed. Never before has a land so affected me. For Africa I had more emotion—a greater wave of understanding and recognition. But China is to the wayfarer of a little week, and I suspect of a little year, incomprehensible. I have of course a theory, an explanation, which brings some vague meaning to the mass of things I have seen and heard. But I know, as I have never known before, that in the face of a people and a human history, I have missed the whole meaning; perhaps even I have missed any significant part. But this I know: any attempt to explain the world, without giving a place of extraordinary prominence to China, is futile. Perhaps the riddle of the universe will be settled in China; and if not, in no part of the world that ignores China.

Peiping

It stands on that great north plain, sweeping up to Siberia and down to the Yangtze Kiang. It is bathed in a cold sunshine. It lies in two great rectangles, with a square within. The square to the north, with vast, grey, massive walls, is the Tartar city. This was a thousand years old when Christ was born, and two thousand years old when Genghis Khan made it his capital. Here the Manchu emperors ruled China from 1618 to 1912, building their power on the magnificence of the Sungs and Mings. Within this Tartar city, and surrounded by pink walls, twenty feet high and occupying two square miles, is the red-walled Forbidden City, which no foreigner entered until 1900. Outside and to the south of the Tartar city, lies the oblong Chinese city, with walls thirty feet high. Within these walls, and walls within walls, dwell a million and a half people on twenty square miles of land, packed with monuments, buildings, towers, arches, tile, porcelain, jewels, inscription, manuscripts, and customs, habits, songs and a strange language that go back and illustrate and explain the history of three hundred million people for four thousand years.

The Chinese City

Nearly everyone has seen some echo or imitation of a Chinese city. There is one in New York; one in Chicago, and a real one in San Francisco. The casual observer might think these imitations, caricatures. But once see Chien Meng street in Peiping, and one knows that this human organism is a typical Chinese invention, age old, rooted in the soul of a people, and expressing as well as any one thing can express, their life and work and play. First of all, it is full of people; it reeks with humanity, it crowds, pushes, swarms. The first day I was in Peiping I must have walked ten miles on this street and its cross alleys. It is a continuous succession of little shops, stores, artisans' markets, personal services. It is commercialism, ingrained, concentrated, complete. It caters to every want of the streaming humanity that eddies through it like an endless flood. In some Negro sections of New Orleans or Charleston there is a faint approach to this situation, but only faint, for this is infinitely older, with a tradition and autonomy which the new Negro city lacks. Perhaps in the Africa of the Middle Age there was something like it. Crowded as are the merchants and purveyors to human want, the buyers, the seekers are more numerous. Someone has said that if the population of Europe were swept away tomorrow, it could be repeopled from China, and yet leave behind in China a population as dense as that of the United States. It is in the sheer weight of its numbers that China must be hearkened to, if for nothing else. Babies, babies, everywhere, and women nowhere, save as mothers, housekeepers and followers of the world's oldest profession.

The Rulers

Above the weltering masses, the rulers and the splendid memory of rulers dead and gone, I have seen the Temple of Heaven—one of the world's most beautiful monuments: the Forbidden City, with its Peacock Throne, its palaces and store of treasure, despite the loot which drunken Europe stole after the Boxer war, and carried away in the name of Christianity. There was the temple of Confucius and the stone classic writings of old China; there was the Lama Monastery of Buddha, and of the statues of the eighteen disciples who brought Buddhism to China (I noted two were black and two were brown). At last two things whose memory lingers: that Summer Palace, which the intrepid Empress Dowager set upon a hill in unearthly splendor. Say what you will of Chinese rulers, past and present—and most all I would say with you—yet when Imperial China passed, there passed a glory from the earth; two deeds were finest of all: that stone faced woman, who laughed at fate and took $20,000,000 set aside for a navy and built a fairy-land, with lake, and marble bridge, and glory-roofed palace, rising one above the other, until they stood above the earth and just beneath the sky, looking down on imperial Peking. She lost an empire, but gained immortality. Then and now, Europe prefers navies.

The Great Wall

I write this standing on the Great Wall of China, with twenty-three centuries beneath my feet. The purple crags of Manchuria lie beyond the valley, while behind are the yellow and brown mountains of China. I have been carried up on the shoulders of four men, and down again, for seventy cents. And here I stand on what has been called the only work of man visible from Mars. It is no mud fence or pile of cobbles. It surpasses that mighty bastion of Constantinople which for so many centuries saved Mediterranean civilization from German barbarism. This is a wall of carefully cut stone, fitted and laid with perfect matching and eternal mortar, from twenty to fifty feet high and twenty-five hundred miles long, built by a million men, castellated with perfect brick, and standing, mute and immutable, for more than two thousand years. Such is China.

China and Japan

I talked so long and said so much about China and Japan a few months ago that I have hesitated to return to the subject. But events have moved swiftly in the East, and we see the forerunners of that great change in the world's center which is going eventually—not, of course, this decade or this century—but eventually to make Asia the center of the world again, which is its natural place.

There were premonitions of the present war between China and Japan when I was in Asia last winter. And what we as American Negroes must understand is the broad outline of the whole thing, and not be unconsciously misled by the propaganda current in America. As I have said several times before, Europe was set to dominate Asia, to enslave its coolies and exploit its natural resources in exactly the same way that they are treating Africa and the South Seas. The rise of Japan frustrated this. She compelled China to treat her on the same terms that China treated the great Western nations, and she stopped the aggression of Russia. And from that time to this she has been determined to achieve her economic independence of the Western world by dominating the policies and resources of China.

The Failure of China

China by her size, by the very magnificence of her history, by her art and philosophy, moved with exasperating indecision and yielded at fatal points, until it became quite clear that England, France and

Germany were going to dominate China and that the only country that could dispute this was Japan. The World War and the Great Depression made it impossible for Europe to pursue her Asiatic plans. Unless, therefore, Japan took advantage of this breathing spell and made herself dominant in China she would surrender China eventually to Europe.

China and Russia

It would have been magnificent providence of God if Russia and China could have made common ground for the emancipation of the working classes of the world. The salvation of China then would not have rested upon Japan, and two-thirds of the world would have been arrayed against the industrial imperialism of Europe. But China, after hesitation, after losing her great and far-sighted leader, Sun Yatsen, turned in reality toward the leadership of modern industrial imperialism as represented in China, especially by England. Japan, therefore, fought Europe by attacking China, and that is the reason of the present war.

The World Attack on Japan

The world attack upon Japan was a subtle thing. Not by battleships or military aggression did Europe seek after the World War to curb this impudent little brown nation. They proceeded to make it difficult, if not impossible, for her to buy raw material in the world. Japan tried to circumvent Europe and America by cheap and efficient manufacture, by a far-flung export campaign. Her success, so long as the depression lasted, was so spectacular that the world grew doubly afraid; but when recovery came they clamped down on manufacture in Japan. Gradually, surely, they raised the price of raw material, of cotton, of iron, of a hundred things which Japanese manufacture must have. There was only one place where Japan could get these things on her own territory, and that was by the annexation of North China, and this she proceeded to accomplish.

War

The only excuse for war is war. It is to escape annihilation and subjection and the nameless slavery of Western Europe that Japan has gone into a horrible and bloody carnage with her own cousin; but the cause and the blame of this war lies on England, and France, and America; on Germany and Italy; on all those white nations, which for a hundred years and more, have by blood and rapine forced their rule upon colored nations. Japan believes that colored nations are going to escape this fate in the future if they organize themselves in self-defense, and when China refused to organize herself, but made herself a part of imperial industry and English and French industrial expansion, Japan seized the opportunity during the paralysis of European power, and undertook this duty herself. It was a terrible effort. It is one of the great deciding wars of the world. And the future of the colored people is bound up with it.

I stood a year ago where that Chinese bomb fell before the Hotel Cathay. I was on those busy corners where other shells killed hundreds in the midst of the International Settlement, and I knew then, as I know now, that the present war in Asia has as its effective cause the African slave trade and the Industrial Revolution in Europe.

The Color of Asia

All this, of course, made Mansart eager to visit Russia, that weird land around which all revolutionary hope and fear were swirling, and thence to pass on for a glance at Asia. He had had Russia in mind when he first began this trip, but he had been advised by friends and people whom he had met in America, England and France that perhaps such a trip would not be wise; that Russia was in turmoil and that no one knew just how things were coming out. So he had given up the idea. But he was going to Asia, and the quickest way to Asia was across Russia by way of the Trans-Siberian railroad. It seemed foolish and too costly for him to go around by the Mediterranean. So he thought that perhaps he could spend a month in Russia and then go on.

This he found out was not possible. For some reason which he could not imagine, he was refused the right to stop in Russia. He did not know about the unfortunate experiences of the Russian Intourist effort; and of the new strains which the West was beginning to put upon this struggling country. So that the best he could do was to make the trip from Moscow into Manchuria without halt. This he finally decided upon. He wrote home as he started east:

"It is October, 1936. I am in Russia. I am here where the world's greatest experiment in organized lifes in the making, whether it fails or not. Nothing since the discovery of America and the French Revolution is of equal importance. And yet this experiment is being made in the midst of unexampled hostility; amid deep-seated bitterness and recrimination such as men reserve usually for crime, degeneracy and blasphemy."

He neared Mongolia and wrote:

"We were nearing Mongolia, and already in the Province of the Buriats. The slim firs stood sturdily with straight heads and shoulders sagging with snow. The lonely silence of a Siberian night was about us. We climbed down a pass in the Black Mountains, following a river half hidden in ice. Suddenly the tempo of the scene changed. A large new factory blazed up in the night. Great piles of lumber lined the river bank. An electric road showed a beginning of modern road-making. Tracks of rails stretched wide on either side, until a modern railway yard was evident. Then we swept, into Vereudinsk, now newly named, and the world was soldiers. They filled the depot, covered the platform, crowded a standing train and marched about in overcoats to their heels, buttoned closely; some with guns, some with bundles. All was now clear. This was a frontier point of concentration against the threat of Japan.

"Ten thousand miles east of our East lies a land, lonely and dust-swept, pregnant with history in the dim past. Hence came the Mongol hordes that swept from Asia to Germany and Italy, and changed the history of the modern world. Brown men they were and yellow, with broad faces and flat noses and wild, straight black hair. They are here about me today, November 1936—perhaps 25,000,000 of them—in Inner and Outer Mongolia and in Manchuria.

"It was a new world. My color was nothing unusual. All the world was sallow, yellow or brown, except the blonde white Russian girls who waited on tables in the restaurants and on the dining car. The train swung out toward the East. I was in a Pullman car made in America. The porter was not of my own expert race, and I felt like giving him a few pointers. The roadbed was better than in Siberia. Always war hovered near us. They pulled down the curtains early. I wanted to look out but fortunately I first read the posted notices: 'Passengers between Hake and Agounor must not look out of the windows on penalty of severe punishment.' I did not look out.

"We swept along a great, wide plain, and the cold wind poured straight down from the North Pole. It was a desolate, barren land, and the seldom folk crept wearily along the lonely way. Then the whole scene changed as if by magic. We slipped out of the desolation of the northern desert. We flew easily on a perfect roadbed, ballasted with rock, and in Japanese cars better than Pullmans. The service was perfect. We were leaving the old border and haunts of the bandits, the modern successors of Genghis Khan. We came to Hsinksing, capital of the new Manchurian state, set up by Japan in 1932.

"I hurried on to China which was end and aim of all imperial planning, from America to Japan and from the tenth century to the twentieth. In the morning I went down to the great harbor of Dairen. My friends handed me three colored streamers of farewell, and following the beautiful Japanese custom I and a dozen others held one end while the friends ashore unwound the other ends until a rainbow of colored strips of paper streamed from ship to shore and I bade Manchukuo goodbye. . . ."

". . . I talked with a group of Chinese leaders and business men. We talked nearly three hours. I plunged in recklessly. I told them of my slave ancestors, of my education and travels; of the Negro problem in America. Then I turned on them and said: 'How far do you think Europe can continue to dominate the world; or how far do you envisage a world whose spiritual center is Asia and the colored races? You have escaped from the domination of Europe politically since the World War—at least in part; but how do you propose to escape from the domination of European capital? How are your working classes progressing? Why is it that you hate Japan more than Europe when you have suffered more from England, France and Germany than from Japan?' "

Mansart wanted to forestall the usual question and comment of foreigners on the Negro problem in America and instead elicit so far as possible information about China from Chinese lips. He continued:

"I saw today something on the streets of your city which reminded me of America. A well-dressed English child of perhaps six years was walking with his nurse along the Bund when he met some Chinese children, small, poorly dressed and dirty. With a gesture he ordered them off the sidewalk; they meekly obeyed and walked in the gutter. In general the whites here treat the Chinese just as we Negroes are treated in the Southern United States. I hear that only recently have Chinese been admitted to the Race Track which is the fashionable amusement center of your city. The white foreigners rule your city, force your children into separate schools and in general act as though they owned China and the Chinese. Why do you permit this?"

In later years, Mansart was deeply ashamed of calling this conference and asking these questions because he came to realize how abysmally ignorant he was of China and her history. He had never studied or read Chinese history or literature. In elementary school, China was a joke and its people "queer." In college he learned about the kings of England and France but nothing of the Han or Ming emperors. At this very moment, in 1936, Mansart had no dream of the frightful tragedy playing over China, or of the "Long March" of 8,000 miles, circling from Fukien to Yunnan, Szechwan and Shenshi. Just then, Chu Teh, of whom Mansart never heard, fleeing from capture in the freezing snows of Tibet, was starting out to join Mao Tsetung in the future Red Capital of Yennan. The long-enslaved, raped and murdered peasants of China were at last reeling to their feet, covered with blood and lice, to rule a world. And yet, of their fateful history of three thousand years and its bloody culmination in the twentieth century, Mansart in his ignorance was questioning Chinese leaders in Shanghai as to why they let the West insult and rule them! They must have wondered whether he was fool or spy.

Of what the West had done to China since 1839, Mansart had heard little—of the Opium Wars to enrich England and reduce China to a colony; of the Chinese revolt called the Taiping "rebellion," in which the whoremonger and murderer, Chinese Gordon, began his saintly career which ended when the Negroes of the Sudan cut off his head; of the slave trade in Chinese coolies which sent cheap labor to America and the second frenzied revolt of the Chinese under the Boxers in 1899, when the Christian world united to steal China's treasures and partition her land. All this was either distorted or utterly unknown to this colored American. When he asked why they submitted to the West, there was a sensible pause quite as awkward for Mansart as for the five Chinese present at the dinner. Mansart remembered how often he had sat in similar quandary when well-meaning strangers had stripped his soul bare in public and blandly asked him why and how and what? Present with him today were five persons–the superintendent of the Chinese elementary schools; the president of a college, supported largely by missionary funds from the United States; a young banker; a well-to-do merchant; and a civil servant.

The school superintendent spoke first. "We are, sir, as you say, in a sense strangers and outcasts in our own land. That we realize each day. But we are not sitting supinely by and doing nothing. Oh, no! Europe is not always going to own and rule Asia. We have started a good system of schools, well supported, with Chinese teachers. There are not enough schools, to be sure, but they are growing. We share today in the government of this city as we did not a decade ago, and there is no longer exclusion of Chinese citizens from public places."

"But," said the merchant, "as you surmise, the chief difficulty is industrial. The Chinese are poor, miserably poor, and crowded into this city in a great hungry mass; foreign capital can easily get work done at the lowest wages and there is yet no effective effort to keep the income of the poor much above starvation. Such unions as we have are ineffective, and the Chinese employers cannot raise wages in face of foreign competition. But we are moving, as our banker can tell you."

"At last," said the banker, "we issue our own money and are not forced to use British currency. That is a start. But of course only a beginning, so long as industry is monopolized by outsiders. They own the factories and ships. But we have plans afoot. Down the river from Shanghai and nearer the sea, we are building a new industrial capital which will one day intercept the world trade which now centers in white-ruled Shanghai. You shall visit it this afternoon."

"Now," began the college president, "about Japan."

He probably sensed that Mansart had the Western prejudice in favor of the Japanese and knew nothing of recent occurrences. Indeed, when Mansart only that very morning had seen the monument erected in 1932 for the Chinese murdered in Chapei by the Japanese, he had not dreamed of what Japan had done to crush China as Sun Yat-sen struggled to free it. Before he left China, Chiang Kai-shek was captured in his night-shirt and made to promise to help China ward off Japan; Mansart knew almost nothing of this man whom our own General Stilwell called "a grasping, bigoted, ungrateful little rattlesnake" but who was given 3 billion dollars of our tax money—to become our "ally" in Formosa.

The president continued: "The Japanese are our kin. We gave them the civilization which they have developed. But today they despise us because we are victims of Western aggression which they barely escaped, and because of their power they propose to replace the West as our masters. It is explicable that we hate so fiercely our own Asiatic brothers who plan to treat us worse than the foreign devils from beyond the seas."

The talk proceeded and food and tea passed. Later the group visited the classes in the public schools where of course no white child entered. At last they came to that new ghost city beside the sea in the wide mouth of the Yangtze River. The marble city hall stood beautiful and empty; there were streets and stores, public buildings and parks, docks and storehouses. Almost everything except people. Mansart stared and wondered. When would the people come? When would the dream awake?

Yet, he also realized that the traveller must take with him much knowledge or he will never see what is before his eyes, or hear with his ears. He knew of British culture before he went to England; he knew much of France before he saw it. But of China what little he knew was mostly distortion. Through that false fog he saw little even when he stood with open eyes.

One of his final days he spent in Hangchow, that lovely city of islands and palatial homes, of tree and verdure, where the wealth of Chinese rests in peace. It was a singular echo of that other great monument at which he but glanced, that magnificent palace of the proud Empress Dowager where, with imperial gesture, this indomitable ruler of hundreds of millions of human beings tossed away the money which her nation gave her for a navy to defend them from the West, and instead built a fairyland of water, bridge and stone, of ebony and ivory, of flower and fountain and vine, of lovely couch and carved statue—to speak of Beauty and never of War.

Across the straits Mansart hurried to Japan, the one colored nation whose talent, industry and military might the white West feared. He looked on the island mountains with intense curiosity. He sensed a difference immediately. In China he had received every courtesy and yet he knew that China felt itself part of a white world and planned its future as part of that world. No sooner had he set foot in Japan than he felt himself in a colored nation who hated the white world just as he, despite all effort, did himself. He was received almost as a fellow-citizen. He again wrote home:

"I have never been welcomed to a land, least of all to my own, as I was welcomed to Japan. I was helped past the port officials, white Americans being politely but firmly elbowed aside, to their open-mouthed surprise. It was astonishing to be at last in a colored country, able and determined to run itself without white advice. And Japan considers itself colored and not white. I have already tested this in conversation and suggestion.

"What is Japan? I am, I admit, prejudiced in its favor. But I am trying to judge it fairly. First of all, it is colored. The blonde-haired world of my summer and fall is gone. The hair of the Japanese is coal black, with once in a thousand a faint brown. The skins vary from white to sallow, and then to yellow and brown. Casually, if I woke up suddenly in Japan, I should imagine myself among New Orleans or Charleston mulattoes.

"But the most extraordinary thing about the Japanese is not physical; it is spiritual. They are independent and self-reliant and self-sufficient colored folk in a world now dominated by whites. They have no fear of white folks nor secret envy. Whatever white folk do or have done, the Japanese are sure they can do better.

"It was the fear of England that was pushing Japan. England dominated China and India, Australia and New Zealand. But for the grace of God and the vigilance of the Japanese, she would own Japan. At one time during and after the Russo-Japanese war, recognizing the power and ability of the Japanese, England made alliance with her as an equal. Then, with no reason except the unstated one of color prejudice in America, South Africa and Australia, Britain broke the alliance in 1921, unwilling to link her fortunes with yellow people.

"Japan found herself between the devil and the deep blue sea; rapprochement with China, based on blood kinship and cultural likeness, was stopped by war and boycott, and reached unbelievable depths of hatred. Japan saw China kow-towing to the West, dragging whites about in human-powered rickshaws; she sensed nothing of the unbreakable strength of China, beneath a thousand years of humility. Europeans secretly and openly encouraged a split between these colored peoples which played directly into their hands. There seemed nothing for Japan to do but seek alliance with Germany and Italy, despite the fact that

Germany despises yellow races and Italy's hands are red with the blood of black Africa.

"There is poverty in Japan; there is oppression; there is no democratic freedom. But nowhere in the modern world is there higher literacy, as newspaper circulations of one, three and even five millions prove. The Japanese laborer is not happy but he is not hopelessly discontented, for he belongs to the same class and family as the highest Japanese. They will guide and protect. He will obey.

"To me, the tragedy of this epoch was that Japan learned Western ways too soon and too well, and turned from Asia to Europe. She had a fine culture, an exquisite art, and an industrial technique miraculous in workmanship and adaptability. The Japanese clan was an effective social organ and her art expression was unsurpassed. She might have led Asia and the world into a new era. But her headstrong leaders chose to apply Western imperialism to her domination of the East, and Western profit-making replaced Eastern idealism. If she had succeeded, it might have happened that she would indeed have spread her culture and achieved a co-prosperity sphere with freedom of soul. Perhaps!"

In the dying days of 1936, while great Fujiyama still veiled its silver face, Mansart went down to Yokohama and set foot upon the sea. He sailed east into the sunset again to discover America, in his own thought and through the thinking and doing of other folk. Ten days he journeyed until he came, at Christmas, to an unbelievable land of raining sunshine and everlasting flowers, called Hawaii.

New Years, 1937, he stood in California of fact and fable, with the city of St. Francis of poverty and the birds before him, and lifted up his eyes to the hills beyond the Golden Gate. Lifted them and let them drop; two small years, two little years; suddenly he saw the whole world again aflame.

A Chronicle of
Race Relations [I]

The Second World War

The outcome of the present war is bound to have large effect upon the theory of races and the relations of the larger cultural groups of mankind. This is not inherently involved in the causes of war and its present development. These causes are based on industrial technique, world commerce, colonial imperialism and the severe and increasing competition of the European empires. But bound up with this today and a bitter emotional drive to action, is the racial theory of Adolph Hitler and the German Nationalist Socialist leaders.

This race theory found its primary motive in Hitler's youthful fixation against Jews; in the economic rivalries and competition between German and Jew in the developments from 1914 to 1933, and primarily in the fact that race hatred proved one of the most effective stimuli on which an emotional appeal to national unity and group revenge could be based. It is not clear, however, how far race theory is going to motivate Germany's action after the war, in her attitudes toward the world. We may assume that her expulsion of the Jews from German life will continue, but her attitude toward Jews elsewhere in the world may conceivably change because of their still great influence and power.

The attitude of Germany toward other colored peoples has long shown signs of racial accommodation: she recognized the Japanese as "Aryan" and has assiduously courted them. It may easily happen that her efforts thoroughly to disintegrate the British Empire will lead to similar recognition of the Indians and Malays. In Africa she will as soon as possible seize her former colonies and quite possibly along with Italy take over other colonial possessions from the English, the French and the Portuguese. She would thus become a ruler of perhaps a majority of black Africans. In such case, however, she would meet rivalry in white South Africa, in English Kenya and in black West Africa, not to mention French Senegal. She could not hold these countries in subjection without considerable recognition of economic rights and even some political autonomy. In fact by granting in British West Africa a greater degree of political autonomy than the English have allowed, Germany could easily make her domination there more secure. On the other hand, any attempt to reduce black Africa to more complete serfdom than she at present suffers, would make the Negroes of the world secret and even open allies of a possible rebirth of British and French power. This would be something for Germany seriously to consider.

We are reminded that a novel by Jules Verne called *The Five Hundred Millions of the Begum* has as its hero Herr Schulze who closely resembles Hitler. He proposes to found a world kingdom upon a theory of race and installs vast machines for destruction. In the end he is a victim of his own invention and when his death is announced, his whole system crumbles.

Albert Bushnell Hart, the venerable historian, predicts that the British Isles will become the next theatre of war; that Germany will land troops in Brazil six months after the end of the European war and that Indians with a million fighting men will expand in Asia.

A dispatch from Europe tells us that the "best shock troops are the Moroccans and Senegalese. The Senegalese are unusually muscular and tall, black as the ace of spades, and usually fanatical in their bravery." This means, of course, that in the present slaughter, as in the first World War, the black troops are being rushed to the front to be killed by German guns and thus save the lives of as large a number as possible of white Europeans.

Race and Culture

Dr. William H. Kilpatrick, in accepting the chairmanship of the executive committee of the Service Bureau for education, made a succinct statement of the present definitions of race and culture which deserves quoting.

> At the outset, we recognize no group characteristics, of a behavior kind, as given or fixed by reason of any alleged "*racial*" or other biological descent. We are not authorized to say that this negative has been scientifically proved. To prove a general negative is a large order. But I believe we can assert:
>   (1) That no such biological origin of existing differences has been proved.
>   (2) That the closer the study, the less grounds appear for believing in "racial" differences of ability or disposition.
>   (3) That an increasing majority of competent scholars disbelieve in such differences.
> For myself, I believe that such alleged biological differences do not exist, at least for any groups that concern us in this country. And I believe I speak for my colleagues when I say that we propose to act on that assumption. The differences that we now find are cultural in origin and so have been learned. There are, to be sure, *individual* differences and of probably many kinds; but group differences, no.
> Where—as seems the case with many Sicilians, Filipinos, and Negroes in our midst—available intelligence tests indicate for these a lower than average I.Q., it is because these members of these groups have had less than average opportunity to learn the culture embodied in the tests. In other words, the reflection is on the tests, or the use made of them, and not on the people thus stigmatized.
> Our country is a nation of varied cultural groups most of whom have come of their own choice to these shores. There is good reason to believe that the constituent variety has, on the whole, tended to build a better total group than would have resulted from any one single origin. The various groups as such may yet contribute to a desirable richness of American life.

Dr. Kilpatrick goes on to discuss the problem of group culture and group segregation within the nation and to ask how far this is advantageous and how far a danger.

Any conscious cultural history is an asset in the life of any group, partly to help maintain the permanence of the group, partly to add to the joy of living of the group. One reason why these things are so is that through and in the cultural history the individual in fact lives. His selfhood expands to identification with his history and he finds joy in feeling its glory and achievements, possibly at times—to be sure—a compensation for meager personal achievement.

This brings a discussion of the definition of "culture" in the sense that it is used today in anthropology.

The anthropological term, the culture, is to be sharply distinguished from the word "culture" in such phrases as "a lady of culture and refinement" or a "cultured gentleman." In such phrases, "culture" means that superior cultivation which naturally results from superior opportunity and leisure.

The anthropological term, the culture, includes all the man-made parts and aspects of the human environment, all those human discoveries and contrivances through the use of which man lives above the beasts; specifically, language, customs, institutions, tools, knowledge, ideals, standards, and the like, through which associated life proceeds. To each defined group belongs its peculiar culture, which in its turn molds the youth of that group to its model. The actual selfhood of each growing child is built on the group ideal as this is incarnate in the family and close community group of that child. It is thus that the so-called "racial" characteristics get built. It is in this way that the lack of comparative opportunity gets in its deadly work for the less fortunate among us. It is because the very selfhood is thus formed that group members hold so tenaciously to group characteristics. It is their own life. These are intertwined with the most sacred memories of childhood. In fact, the culture defines the group rather than the other way about.

There follows a discussion of the question as to how far this group culture is consistent with a national culture.

The problems of this organization seem to group themselves into two heads:
  (1) The theoretical problem of what degree of differentiation is right and proper for any sub-group to maintain with the larger whole.
  (2) The practical problem of helping to maintain the just rights of minority groups as over against the unjust and unfair demands and treatment of others.

A glance at each is as far as we can here and now go. As to the permissible and proper degree of difference which a sub-group may maintain: Modern society is increasingly interdependent. A certain degree of effective internal solidarity is therefore necessary for the welfare alike to the total group and of the concentrated numbers. Specifically, in this country we must have at least enough internal solidarity to secure

(1) shared discussion of public policy problems
(2) free voting
(3) and effective execution of the legal and other governmental machinery.

If, however, we were to stop on the legalistic note above sounded, the discussion would have missed an essential point. Man cannot live on rights alone. Mere legal enforcement of legally defined rights, cannot afford a sufficient basis for common living. There must be mutual respect, and mutual good will, and if possible mutual understanding and a fair amount of mutual admiration. Otherwise, difficulties and misunderstandings and mutual hatreds will arise. Political blocs will result. Distrust will grow, and demagogs abound. Each group owes it to the rest to try to live on a higher degree than mere legal definition of rights. "Dominant" groups have peculiar obligations to take the first and leading steps toward good and just relations; and "minority" groups owe their correlative duties not to foster needlessly irritating differences.

An Inter-American Congress has met in Mexico for ten days with official delegates from twenty-one American republics. Its object is to study problems of the Indian populations of America. It established headquarters in Mexico for an inter-American Institute for Indian Study, and appointed a permanent committee to direct those studies. The resolutions adopted by the Congress included one to help Indians in acquiring farms in countries where it is difficult for them to get land and to be furnished credit and technical help. A Pan-American Bank for Agricultural Credit was suggested. Other resolutions suggested that Indian customs and special circumstances affecting Indians be taken into consideration in enacting and applying laws, and that Indian women have equal property rights with men. The celebration of a "Day of the Indian" was recommended throughout the American continent.

Europe

The Soviet census of 1939 shows that 81.2 per cent of the population can now read and write. In 1926 the literacy was 51 per cent. Of the present population, nearly 9 per cent has had secondary school training and six-tenths of one per cent university training. There are forty-nine recognized nationalities in Russia, among which are three million Jews. The decrease in illiteracy is in itself an astonishing accomplishment.

Three years ago Sir Herbert Samuel blamed France and England for their present plight because they had refused to support the League of Nations and stand up strongly against Italian aggression in Ethiopia:

> Today we see the result: Spain, Austria, Czechoslovakia, Poland, Finland, Norway have all become victims of ruthless aggression, but it still remains a cold and stubborn fact that Ethiopia was the first—first lamb of the sacrifice—because when she was attacked, she was bare of modern means of warfare, and forsaken by those who were bound by sacred pledge to help her.

In April an exhibit of France Overseas was opened in Paris by the Minister of Colonies. In the Grand Palais prepared for this exhibit the visitor makes a voyage over the world and sees conditions in Indo-China, Algeria, Tunis, Morocco, French West Africa, French Equatorial Africa, Madagascar and the autonomous colonies. There is a special exposition of the work of colonial troops. The banners of these troops since 1622 are exhibited and their movements and battles traced. Colonial art in carpets, cloth, metal, jewelry, wood and ceramics is exhibited and French manufacturers show the goods which they are making for colonial consumption. Soldiers and workers from the colonies can pass their time here in special recreation rooms when on leave. Broadcasts on the greatness and wealth of the French colonial empire are heard from lime to time.

The medical director general of the service of health in French West Africa reports that the health of black soldiers is excellent and the camps in which they are concentrated satisfactory from the hygienic point of view; especially are the riflemen well-lodged and well-fed and the sickness is less than in 1939.

France has just made Galandou Diouf, the black deputy from Senegal, an officer in the Legion of Honor. Like his predecessor, Blaise Diagne in the first War, Diouf has recruited thousands of native soldiers and has worked among the black troops now on the Western Front. Diouf is a man of huge stature and a Mohammedan with three wives and nine children. He became a lieutenant and won the *Croix de Guerre* in the first World War.

Ásia

Tadataka Ikesaki, writing in the *Nippon Hyóron* in December, 1939, discusses the speech of Ambassador Joseph C. Grew, "straight from the horse's mouth":

> Of course, we know that our relations with the United States have not been smooth. We witnessed the sudden abrogation of the Commercial Treaty. We saw a unit of the American fleet dispatched to Hawaii without any revealed reason. Thus, we wondered why the United States has acted in such an annoying and suspicious manner toward us. But we have never thought that war between the United States and Japan is inevitable.
>
> People of America! Let us also speak "straight from the horse's mouth": the attitude which you have maintained toward Japan since the Manchurian Incident has not been pleasant to the Japanese. We often felt irritated. But we have always and at all times exercised our characteristic reserve. We replied to your selfish irresponsible words and acts with over-politeness

and self-restraint. With our utmost efforts we are trying to correct your misunderstandings.

Therefore, *as far as the people of Japan are concerned*, we have never thought of cutting off our ties with you. Nor have we ever thought of fighting with you. But when we learned, in the words of your ambassador, that you seemed to have been anxiously thinking quite contrary to us on the subject, then we ask you: Are you, on your part, thinking of fighting with Japan?

Recently there have been indications that America's intransigent attitude may be softened with the possibility of German victory, especially as her fleet will be needed in the Atlantic rather than in the Pacific.

The Dutch East Indies consists of Java and Madura with 51,000 square miles and forty-eight millions of people; Sumatra, with 163,000 square miles and ten millions of people; and a multitude of other islands aggregating 521,000 square miles and twelve millions of people. Here is an area fifty-eight times as large as the Netherlands and inhabited by seventy million colored people.

They raise material primarily for European consumption, consisting of a million and a half tons of sugar, nearly 40 per cent of all the rubber raised in the world, nearly 20 per cent of all the tin, and sixty million barrels of petroleum. For their own support they raise nine million tons of rice. These islands are, of course, Asiatic and near Japan and their products vital to her existence; yet the United States and Europe, thousands of miles away, are warning Japan not to touch them. It is as though Japan should warn the United States from interference with Cuba. Japan on her part has cried "hands off" to Europe and America.

The Philippine Islands are restricting immigration to five hundred persons a year from any other country. This would cut down the immigration of Japanese and Chinese. No yellow people can migrate to white Australia, the United States or Europe. On the other hand white Europeans and Americans can migrate to any part of the world and demand preferential treatment. Facts like these increase racial and cultural friction.

India

A clear statement of the question of minorities in India is made in a pamphlet recently issued by the All-India Congress Committee:

> What is this minority question which is being exploited by the British Government? Muslims are not a minority throughout India. In several provinces they form a majority of the population. In the whole of India, Muslims are not a political, national or ethnic minority. They are not a community in the political sense of the term. A Muslim in the Punjab is a Punjab as the Punjab premier is rightly proud to proclaim himself to be. One from Bengal is a Bengali and from Sindh is a Sindhi. Every Muslim in India belongs to one or the other historical sub-nationalities of India. The Muslims are, therefore, a religious group just like Hindus, Jain, Sikhs, Indian Christians, etc. As such they with justice claim safeguards for the protection of their religion, culture, language, script and even their personal law. They can also claim a fair share in public administrative appointments. All this has been repeatedly guaranteed by the Congress. Their participation in political office cannot, however, be based upon their religion, but only upon their being Indians and holding particular political opinions, and advocating political and economic policies. No minority can be allowed to stand in the way of the political and economic advance of the country. If religious denominations have their rights, political majorities too have their rights. It has never been recognized as one of the rights of denominational minorities or for that matter of any minority in a democracy, to exercise a veto over the will of the nation to freedom and self-determination. India has several religious minorities. Is every one of them to have a right to thwart the will of the nation, or is exception to be made only in favour of the Muslim League?
>
> As a matter of fact, the British Government have left no majority in India. According to it the Muslims are a minority, the scheduled castes are a minority, the Sikhs, Parsis, Indian Christians, Anglo-Indians, Europeans, the princes are all minorities, nay even women are a minority. The non-Brahmans and the Marhattas are minorities. The only majority left are the Brahmans bereft of their women folk. Arithmetic is out of place in this imperial calculation. But minority rights have never stood in the way, whenever England has been obliged to part with power. It did not allow minority considerations to weigh with her while conceding self-determination to South Africa, though the war with the Boers was ostensibly fought for the protection of the minorities. But it appears that

principles that are good for the rest of the British Empire are not good enough for India.

The fifty-third session of the Indian National Congress met March 19 and 20, 1940.

The Ramgarh session of the Congress met under the Presidentship of Maulana Abul Kalam Azad in a large, open and tastefully decorated amphitheatre formed by the natural undulations of the ground. Just as the session was about to commence—5:30 p.m.—there was a heavy downpour of rain upsetting all the arrangements. Soon there was a deluge. The delegates and visitors, however, stuck to their places. When they could sit no longer, they stood up in knee-deep water. At the appointed hour, in continuing rain, the proceedings commenced. Babu Rajendra Prasad, the Chairman of the Reception Committee, extended a welcome to the delegates and thanked them and the visitors for keeping to their places, defying the weather. Maulana Abul Kalam Azad then addressed the audience. He said the task before the country must be finished through rain, flood and storm. The fight for freedom must continue under all circumstances. He congratulated them on the courage and discipline shown by them in keeping to their places, determined to see through the work of the day.

The presidential address said, among other things:

For a hundred and fifty years British Imperialism has pursued the policy of divide and rule, and by emphasizing internal differences, sought to use various groups for the consolidation of its own power. That was the inevitable result of India's political subjection, and it is folly for us to complain and grow bitter. A foreign government can never encourage internal unity in the subject country, for disunity is the surest guarantee for the continuance of its own domination. But when we were told, and the world was asked to believe, that British Imperialism had ended, and the long chapter of Indian history dominated by it had closed, was it unreasonable for us to expect that British statesmen would at last give up this evil inheritance and not exploit the communal situation for political ends? But the time for this is yet distant; we may not cling to such vain hopes. So the last five months with their succession of events have established. Imperialism in spite of all assurances to the contrary, still flourishes; it has yet to be ended. . . .

Today even in the middle of the twentieth century, we witness how the new reactionary forces in Europe have shattered man's faith in individual and collective human rights. In place of justice and reason, brute force has become the sole argument in the determination of rights. But while the world is presenting this depressing picture, there is another side, the hopeful side, which cannot be ignored. We see countless millions all over the world, without any distinction, awakening to a new consciousness which is spreading everywhere with great rapidity. This new consciousness is tired of the utter hopelessness of the old order, and is impatient for a new order based on reason, justice and peace. This new awakening which arose after the last war and took root in the deepest recesses of the human soul, has now come to dominate men's minds and their utterances. Perhaps there is no parallel in history to the speed of this awakening.

Mahatma Gandhi made two speeches and said, among other things:

With me there is no other alternative than non-violence. If you feel that you are to fight and you must fight now and immediately and feel convinced that there is some other method of winning the fight, I would ask you to go ahead and I shall be the first to applaud your victory. But if you do not want to leave me and still you are not prepared to follow my methods and instructions, I would like to know what kind of generalship is this that you offer me. Those who clamor for immediate fight want to have me with them. Why? Because they are conscious that the masses are with me. I unhesitatingly say that I am the people's man. Every moment of my life I feel for the starving millions. I live and am prepared to lay my life down to relieve their sufferings. I have been a faithful servant of theirs. Even if you stone me to death I will still work for the masses. This is my way. If you think there is any other way, please leave me alone. Remember if we, who are assembled here, blunder, we shall cause untold suffering to the dumb millions. You, therefore, bear a heavy responsibility, and as your General my responsibility is still greater. As a General I have to be a sort of beacon-light to you and warn you against any possible disaster. . . .

All the sermons we have had today against British Imperialism will not help you to remove it. They will only make you angry. Anger is opposed to Satyagraha. We have no quarrel with the British people. We want to be their friends and retain their goodwill, not on the basis of their domination over us, but on the basis of a free and equal India. As a free country India will bear no malice to any one, nor attempt to enslave any people. We shall march with the rest of the world, just as we shall desire the rest of the world to march with us.

Satyagraha is the path of truth at all costs. If you are not prepared to follow this path, please leave me alone. You can pronounce me worthless and I shall not resent it. Truth and Ahimsa are the essence of Satyagraha, and Charkha is their symbol. Without full faith in truth, non-violence and the Charkha, you cannot be my soldiers. If you do not believe in this you can leave me alone and find your own methods.

PART III

World War II
and the
Anticolonial
Turn

Du Bois's analysis of World War II as a
race war, a war of imperial rivalry and colonial subjection, became
sharper, angrier, and deeper as the war moved on. So, too, deepened
his conviction that events in Asia were central to the alignment and
direction of the postwar world. This section opens with two essays
written and published in 1942 and 1944, respectively, which demonstrate this movement in Du Bois's thought. In 1942, Du Bois again
used his "A Chronicle of Race Relations" column in *Phylon* to survey
a range of perspectives on the war bound together by a common
thread: criticism of jingoistic nationalism and the consolidation of
western wealth and power. Du Bois cited a host of "mainstream"
sources, Vice-President Henry Wallace, Pearl S. Buck, Australian
Sir Bertram S. B. Stevens, *Fortune* magazine, and the *New York Times*
to muster a case that the war was being used to isolate Asia, especially
Russia and China, while deepening the economic and political crisis
in India. As he had in 1937, Du Bois continued to perceive Japanese
imperialism as a nexus or crossroads of competing and debilitating
political contradictions. "The threat of Japan lies over India and is

111

regarded in two ways:" he wrote. "The Indians say that they cannot organize Indian opposition to Japan if England insists on white supremacy in India; the English say that Japan is so threatening that they cannot give up their grip on India." The essay sees no relief to this impasse in the arrogant indifference of western imperial leadership; it describes the "problem" of the world color line as urgent but unsolvable.

Two years later, Du Bois advanced a more concretized analysis and proposed resolution to the problem of war. In 1944, Du Bois spoke on the topic "Prospect of a World Without Racial Conflict." It made plain a global theory of white supremacy as the driving force of the war's disaster: "The supertragedy of this war is the treatment of the Jews in Germany" he wrote. "There has been nothing comparable to this in modern history. Yet its technique and its reasoning have been based upon a race philosophy similar to that which has dominated both Great Britain and the United States in relation to colored people." Significantly, Du Bois zeroed in on Asia, not Eastern Europe, Africa or Germany, as the central site of the world struggle for racial equality. "The greatest and most dangerous race problem today is the problem of relations between Asia and Europe: the question as to how far 'East is East and West is West' and of how long they are going to retain the relation of master and serf." The essay used colonial India as the baseline for assessing the possibilities and necessities of a radical transformation in what Du Bois called "modern colonial imperialism." Indeed India was perceived as a kind of tipping point for successful challenge to racial supremacy and capitalist inequalities in the postwar period. Du Bois described this challenge in terms indicative of the increasingly materialist cast of his thought: "(1) defense against aggression; (2) full employment after the war; (3) eventual fair distribution of both raw materials and manufactured goods; (4) abolition of poverty; and (5) health." Du Bois was in 1944 beginning to outline a social and political program that he refused to name but which would occupy much of his more nuanced writing on the world color line for the remaining nineteen years of his life.

The remaining selections in this section suggest some of the Asian sources to which Du Bois turned in the development of this program. The first is a brief book review of a biography of Jawaharlal Nehru. Next to Gandhi, Nehru drew more praise from Du Bois than almost any anticolonial leader. He was fascinated by Nehru's commitment to democratic principles, what he calls in the essay "government by the consent of the people and for the integrity of the individual." Du Bois also saw "astonishing resemblances" between English colonialism and the "Negro problem" in America, specifically "the violence, the stress upon religious submission, the inner difficulties within the Indian race and the way in which these difficulties have been played upon to the advantage of the English." Du Bois held Nehru in similar esteem to Sun Yat-sen as visionary nationalists dedicated to building the necessary political apparatus to effect autonomous rule. Finally, Nehru's tolerance for socialism and Communism and his efforts to recast it within India's home rule strategies can be seen as a model of Du Bois's similar efforts in application to black America.

That essay is followed by perhaps Du Bois's most complete essay on the history of Indian liberation struggle. "The Freeing of India" first appeared in the October 1947 *Crisis*, mere months after the country gained independence. It is a kind of primer for *Crisis* readers of the events leading up to August 15. It is a sweeping review of Indian history, religion, and ethnic sects, on one hand, and the country's relationship to neighbors, allies, and political foes. The twin problems facing the country, in Du Bois's view, are Hindu–Muslim strife and the legacy of colonial imperialism. It is ultimately a hopeful essay, reminiscent of the almost utopian desire Marx and Engels felt when they perceived the possibility of Asian liberation from capital in the mid nineteenth century. Likewise, the essay is yet another example of Du Bois measuring the fate of European capitalism by events in Asia. Indeed prior to the decolonization movements of the 1950s in Africa, Du Bois had virtually no examples, outside of Russia, about which he remained ambivalent, of where a colored people's revolution—led by colored people—might succeed. "The Freeing of India" urges the colored world to use India as her example.

India's successful revolution also culminated in his own mind Du Bois's long and impassioned devotion to the life and work of Mahatma Gandhi. More than any African or African American leader, it is Gandhi who qualifies as Du Bois's most passionately admired statesman and activist of the twentieth century. Du Bois, who avoided "great men" readings of history, wrote at least a dozen essays all or in part on Gandhi's work. Next to Lenin, who he often praised with one hand of anti-Communist suspicion behind his back, and Mao, who mystified him, Gandhi was the most accessible prototype of an effective race rebel. There is also a bit of hero identification for Du Bois in Gandhi: the two were born nineteen months apart; Gandhi's work in South Africa was the first evidence Du Bois said he gained of "the tragedy of that awful land." In this relatively brief essay, Du Bois enumerates how Gandhi's nonviolent tactics became, and should continue to become, a useful weapon for black American civil rights struggle. The essay was published in 1957 after Martin Luther King, Jr., had already publicly adopted nonviolence as his southern strategy for change. Du Bois and King's shared admiration for Gandhi has not been sufficiently marked. Nor have their fairly different uses of Gandhi's thought. For King, nonviolence was famously the strategy underlying the Birmingham bus boycotts and most of the major protests of his public life. Gandhi was first and foremost for King a strategist and tactician. For Du Bois, Gandhi was an intellectual compass to colonialism and his opposition to nuclear testing and South African apartheid. Indeed as we will see in the final section of this book, Du Bois clung to Gandhi throughout his life as a symbolic avatar of transnational cooperation, peace, harmony, and moral example. This essay ends with Du Bois's blunt assessment that black American civil rights struggle will not achieve its own freedom dreams until an American Gandhi is born. Interestingly, Martin Luther King's living example was for Du Bois necessary but not yet sufficient to realizing freedom within and without U.S. borders.

The section concludes appropriately with a prescient essay synthesizing Du Bois's analysis and aspirations for the postwar period. "Colonialism, Democracy, and Peace after the War" was written at the invitation of the Haitian government for presentation at a scholarly conference in Haiti in the summer of 1944. The essay begins by defining the "colonial" as inclusive of black Americans in the U.S. The essay then surveys the extant states of colonialism around the globe and notes its cornerstone: white domination of nonwhite. "What now can be done about this," writes Du Bois, in a perhaps conscious echo of Lenin, "in this day of crisis, when with the end of a horrible and disgraceful war in sight, we contemplate Peace and Democracy? What has Democracy to do with Colonies and what has skin-color to do with Peace?" The essay forecasts Du Bois's preeminent concerns in the postwar period, namely aligning a politics of international solidarity across Asia and Africa with the struggles of black Americans in the U.S.

Publication History for Part III

"A Chronicle of Race Relations." *Phylon*, V. 3, n. 4 (1942): pp. 417–34.

"Prospect of a World Without Racial Conflict." *American Journal of Sociology*, V. 49 (March 1944): pp. 450–56.

"Nehru." *Phylon*, V. 4, n. 1, (1943): pp. 89–91.

"Gandhi and the American Negroes." *Gandhi Marg*. V. 1, n. 3 (July 1957): pp. 1–4.

"The Colonial Groups in the Postwar World." In *Against Racism: Unpublished Essays, Papers, Addresses, 1887–1961*. Ed. Herbert Aptheker. Amherst: University of Massachusetts Press, 1985, pp. 229–42.

A Chronicle of
Race Relations [II]

The Wavering Ideals of War

The declared objects of the present World War have changed in essential particulars since the last issue of *Phylon*. It looked then as though this might become openly and declaredly a war for racial and cultural equality. Certain statements since then, tend to support this point of view. The greatest single pronouncement was that by Vice-President Henry A. Wallace, May 8, 1942, in which he said with great frankness

> This is a fight between a slave world and a free world. Just as the
> United States in 1862 could not remain half slave and half free, so in
> 1942 the world must make its decision for a complete victory one way or
> the other. . . .
>   The people are on the march toward even fuller freedom than the most
> fortunate peoples of the earth have hitherto enjoyed. . . .
>   Some have spoken of the "American Century." I say that the century
> on which we are entering—the century which will come out of this war—
> can be and must be the century of the common man. Perhaps it will be
> America's opportunity to suggest the freedoms and duties by which the
> common man must live. Everywhere the common man must learn to
> build his own industries with his own hands in a practical fashion.
> Everywhere the common man must learn to increase his productivity so
> that he and his children can eventually pay to the world community all
> that they have received. No nation will have the God-given right to exploit
> other nations. Older nations will have the privilege to help younger
> nations get started on the path to industrialization but there must be
> neither military nor economic imperialism.

To this Pearl Buck's collected essays called *American Unity and Asia* add in her letter to colored Americans

> If democracy did not win, the white people would have to make themselves into a great standing army, highly trained, constantly prepared to keep the colored peoples subdued, and there could be no greater slavery than that necessity. It is possible, in this grave moment, that in such a place as Australia there might be white people made slaves by their conquerors, just as white people now are slaves in certain countries and no less slaves because their rulers are other white men. The issue today is not one of race, colored or white. It is freedom.

Even some Australian leaders seem to see light. Sir Bertram S. B. Stevens said at Sidney, July 19

> The defeat of Japan is essential if the East is to work harmoniously and amicably with the rest of the world, but the defeat of Japan will not mean a return in the East to the old quiescent subservience.
>
> Europeans and Americans will have to regard the Chinese, Indians, Malays and Javanese as friends of equal status. The days of colonial wars and of making profits by teaching Asiatics the wonders of Western civilization are gone forever.

Mr. Justice Frankfurter of the Supreme Court, speaking at the College of the City of New York, said that we had for a while regarded this war as a war of clashing imperialisms

> Now we see it for what it is—not at all as a war to save either the old British Empire or the new British Commonwealth of Nations. It is a war to save civilization itself from submergence.

On the other hand the imperial tradition will not down. The re-publication of Mackinder's *Democratic Ideals and Reality* emphasizes that there is one continent, the Eastern Hemisphere

> That hemisphere contains fourteen-sixteenths of the human race; England, Japan and the Asiatic islands contain one-sixteenth, with the American island (or islands) covering another sixteenth.

Within this continent lies the heartland and

Who rules East Europe commands the Heartland:
Who rules the Heartland commands the World-Island:
Who rules the World-Island commands the World.

Fortune, the American rich man's magazine, lays down an elaborate plan detailing just how Japan is to be captured, garrisoned and held. All this relapse to imperialism brings the question of future police power. *World Federation Now* says

> A voluntary world "police force" might be better than chaos, provided such force were established and left standing (as in the founding of our United States) without any specific authority to coerce a state. But most writers on international "police force" call for definite provisions authorizing the "police force" to "crack down" on a delinquent state. Such a provision is simply making a Civil War inevitable by putting down in black and white exactly how it shall start.

Former Ambassador Grew who helped on the present war by his remarks "straight from the horse's mouth," which the Japanese must have regarded as adding to a series of national insults, now emphasizes Japanese power

> We are up against a powerful fighting machine, a people whose morale cannot and will not be broken even by successive defeats, who will certainly not be broken by economic hardships, a people who individually and collectively will gladly sacrifice their lives for their Emperor and their nation, and who can be brought to earth only by physical defeat, by being ejected physically from the areas which they have temporarily conquered or by the progressive attrition of their naval power and merchant marine which will finally result in cutting off their homeland from all connection with and access to those outlying areas—by complete defeat in battle.

There is no mention of any attempt to meet whatever justice there is in Japanese demands. The correspondents of the New York *Times* have published fantastic stories of Japan's dreams of world conquest;

but the real difficulty is emphasized by Professor Kennedy of Yale. Asserting that Japan's policy could not be described as seeking the subjugation of the other people of Asia, he said:

> That is only a by-product, and fundamentally it means aligning the yellow race against the white.
>
> The full significance can only be appreciated if you know the intense resentment that has been built up, not only in Japan, but also in China, by a half century of domineering whites.

Colonel Blimp, the British cartoon creation of the war, says

> Gad, sir, Japan is right. Keeping the white man out of the black man's country is the yellow man's burden.

A Negro American soldier adds to this idea when, according to Horace R. Cayton in the *Nation*, he reports a young black recruit as saying

> Just carve on my tombstone, "Here lies a black man killed fighting a yellow man for the protection of a white man."

One element in the war which annoys both Great Britain and America, is that Russia is not fighting Japan, nor is Japan fighting Russia. American newspapers have been filled with the idea that Japan might attack Russia; but Victor A. Yakhontoff says in the *New Republic* that this is but wishful thinking and that the neutrality pact between Tokyo and Moscow shows every likelihood of remaining in force.

> The Russians might even consider it as a part payment for all they had done for us and for the rest of the United Nations by killing more Germans and destroying more of their tanks, airplanes and other war machines than all the other allies, to paraphrase the words of President Roosevelt.

This brings the tragic position of Russia to the fore. There is widely current belief that Russia is not receiving fair consideration from the

United Nations. The public believed that Russia had been promised a second front this year. It seems clear that Churchill's widely advertised visit to Stalin was to tell him frankly that no such help could be expected in 1942. Periodicals like the *New Republic* question the wisdom of this disappointing decision. Bruce Bliven writes

> If in the autumn of 1942, Britain and America are not able to fight one-fifth of Germany's army, how do they expect to fight five-fifths of it—as they may be forced to do—in 1943?

Under the dominant leadership of Churchill neither Russia nor China is a real colleague in the United Nations and this brings us to the tragedy of India.

India

The main cause of the worsening in war ideals in the last few months, is the present situation in India. One cannot be reminded too often that, as Louis Fischer says in the *Nation*, "the poverty and stagnation of India are the background against which the present situation must be seen. . . . India is a miserably poor, hungry, retarded country. Most Indians are half-starved and three-fourths naked."

As Nehru insists in his article in the New York *Times*

> However this war may develop, whatever the end may be, no matter what the peace is going to be, it is certain that the Western World can no longer dominate over Asia. If this is not realized and if the attempt is made to continue the old relationship in any form, this means the end of peace and another disastrous conflict.

The difficulty is that England not only refuses to be held responsible to any serious degree for present social conditions in India but insists that the chief difficulties lie with the Indians themselves and that her broad and adequate promises of eventual Indian independence have been foolishly rejected. On the other hand, the president of the Indian National Congress declared that Cripps did not keep his word.

> You told me then that there would be a national government which would function as a Cabinet and that the position of the Viceroy would be analogous to that of the King of England vis-a-vis his Cabinet. In regard to the India Office [headed by Leopold S. Amery in London] you told me that you were surprised that no one had so far mentioned this important matter, and that the practical course was to have this attached or incorporated with the Dominions' Office.

No sooner had the English power in India heard of this offer than they forced its change and practical annulment. The final offer left the viceroy supreme, the Indians with no real voice in the present government and the future status to depend entirely upon England after the war.

It goes without saying that the Indians do not trust the word of Englishmen. This explains not only the Indian situation but the Irish complication. No amount of protestation on the part of the English can today convince Eire that it can expect honest treatment from England. It is not an answer to this when the English declare that the Indians are already represented in Indian government; that nine of the thirteen members of the Viceroy's Council are Indians. The Indians answer that the Viceroy can veto any action of his Council and that the nine Indians nominated to membership are stooges. A dispatch to the New York *Times* says

> Last Sunday evening in the native section of Old Delhi, some of these sympathizers organized a procession in which the Viceroy was represented by an Indian in tattered clothes and the Indian members of his Council by as many donkeys, with their names on placards, just so that there would be no misunderstanding. It represented one expression of popular feeling.
>
> The gap between those Indians who serve the government and those who are fighting for independence is just as unbridgeable at present as the gap between the British and the Indians.

It is this situation of unbelief and lack of faith that points out the dangers of the present situation. Herbert L. Matthews writes to the New York *Times* saying

> It must always be stressed that mutual distrust is one of the roots of India's troubles and that while Americans take for granted that the British are perfectly sincere and, anyway, could not escape fulfilling their promises even if they wanted to, a great many Indians do not believe them.

There is in this devil's broth the tremendous advantage of having the leadership of Mohandas Gandhi. Despite the slurs of Churchill and the contempt of many Americans, here is one of the world's great men. Lord Linlithgow, Viceroy of India, himself has said "Gandhi is the biggest thing in India." Yet it was Gandhi who moved toward a final break with England. He did it clearly and openly and wrote this resolution for the Indian Congress

> Whereas the British War Cabinet proposals by Sir Stafford Cripps have shown up British imperialism in its nakedness as never before, the All-India Congress Committee has come to the following conclusions:
> The committee is of the opinion that Britain is incapable of defending India. It is natural that whatever she does is for her own defense. There is the eternal conflict between Indian and British interest. It follows that their notions of defense would also differ.
> The British Government has no trust in India's political parties. The Indian Army has been maintained up till now mainly to hold India in subjugation. It has been completely segregated from the general population, who can in no sense regard it as their own. This policy of mistrust still continues, and is the reason why national defense is not entrusted to India's elected representatives.
> Japan's quarrel is not with India. She is warring against the British Empire. India's participation in the war has not been with the consent of the representatives of the Indian people. It was purely a British act. If India were freed, her first step would probably be to negotiate with Japan.

The Congress, at the motion of Nehru, modified the statement concerning Japan so that the resolution finally said "A free India would

know how to defend herself in event of any aggressor attacking her."
The words make little difference, for what rankles in the Indian's mind
is that they are at war today with Japan by declaration of England with
absolutely no consultation with the Indians.

The movement of Gandhi and the Congress was in a sense forced
by Indian public opinion. Gandhi said

> I know full well that the British will have to give us our freedom when we
> have made sufficient sacrifices and proven our strength. We must remove
> the hatred for the British from our hearts. At least in my heart there is no
> such hatred. As a matter of fact, I am a greater friend of the British now
> than I ever was.
>
> The reason for this is that at this moment they are in distress. My
> friendship demands that I must make them aware of their mistakes.
> As I am not in the position in which they find themselves, I am able to
> point their mistakes out to them.
>
> I know they are on the brink of the ditch, and are about to fall into it.
> Therefore, even if they want to cut off my hands, my friendship demands
> that I should try to pull them out of that ditch. This is my claim, at which
> many people may laugh, but all the same, I say this is true.

Evidence of this is widespread. A journalist speaking to Louis Fischer
at the Bombay Journalist Association said "for us Indians there is no
difference between British fascism and Japanese or German fascism."
The threat of Japan lies over India and is regarded in two ways:
the Indians say that they cannot organize Indian opposition to Japan
if England insists on white supremacy in India; the English say that
Japan is so threatening that they cannot give up their grip on India.
The reaction of the English to Gandhi's non-violent revolt has been
peculiar. In the first place it must be remembered that the violence is
not on Gandhi's program. Indeed he has often threatened to starve
himself to death if violence was the result of his program of non-
cooperation. Not violence but non-cooperation is the Gandhi program. But the English make no distinction. Henry Judd declares in
Labor Action that seven hundred and twenty-one Indians have been
killed and one thousand two hundred and nineteen wounded. The

English largely approve this. Churchill's speech was cynical and reactionary to the last degree and simply carries out his long program of opposition to Indian autonomy. Public whipping is permitted and miscellaneous spraying of civilian population by machine guns from airplanes was applauded in Parliament.

More than this we do not know. It is reported that U. Saw, the Burmese Prime Minister and leader, who dared ask Churchill face to face last year for autonomy, is dead after his arrest by the British. The strike of fifty thousand workers at the Tata Munitions Works was not reported in the press for a month and American newspaper men have been bitter at the refusal to allow them to tell the truth.

The greatest result of the break and the most indefensible is the imprisonment of Gandhi, Nehru and other leaders. These men have already spent a large part of their lives in British jails and it is the most contradictory result of the war that men of high character and education who have made their career the fight for democracy, should be imprisoned by the country which is supposed to represent democracy at its highest.

The argument that India cannot be allowed freedom until she settles her internal difficulties is astonishing when it comes from Europeans. That there will be innumerable and serious internal problems which a free India will have to settle; that they may even lead to civil war is quite possible; but that Europe or any European nation should be allowed to settle India's problems for her or to say when India shall be allowed to begin her own settlement, is an inadmissible conclusion.

The reaction of the Indian situation in the United States has been on the whole gratifying. A few influential Americans, to be sure, have stood back of the English attitude and have maintained that America has no interest in this internal problem of the British Empire but the *New Republic* says

From the assumption that India is England's private affair, we have gone ahead, under the false sense of unity, to assume that loyalty to the United

Nations means loyalty to England, and loyalty to England in the India question means loyalty to the English Tories, and loyalty to the English Tories means loyalty to Amery. Consequently, the whole American press has interpreted unity of the United Nations as the duty to follow the Cripps-Amerite version of the Indian situation, and accepts even such gratuitous and basically false propaganda as the smudge on Gandhi as "an appeaser," which both Cripps and Amery know is false. This attitude of accepting wartime lies in the heat of controversy is unworthy of Americans, for the Indians are fighting for what Americans achieved in their Revolutionary War—freedom from England.

Mrs. John Gunther writes bitterly

The biggest and barest case of aggression in the world today is the English aggression in India.

This is the precedent for all other aggressions that have since followed. And until it is wiped out, it will remain the moral and physical excuse for all other aggressions which continue to follow in its rutted trail. . . .

What Britain is doing to India is not only political immorality, it is political lunacy. Not all the perfumes of Araby, nor the most complicated apologies of the subtlest Ministries of Information can cover up that blot.

This war must be fought with planes, guns, and ships, but first of all it must be fought with clean hands.

Robert R. Reynolds, chairman of the Military Affairs Committee of the House of Representatives breaks his record of being wrong on most questions by saying

If we are fighting for the right of people to maintain the government they desire, we can convince the people of the world of our seriousness and good faith only by requiring our ally, Britain, to grant immediate independence to the 370,000,000 people of India.

Oswald Garrison Villard says in the *Times*

What we are witnessing in India is just one more clash between right and expediency, but this war has produced no more piteous tragedy and none more dangerous. It really seems as if democracy were to be slain by the blunders and folly of those who feel themselves to be its most devoted defenders. . . .

From the very beginning of the war in Asia there has been the greatest danger that this struggle would degenerate into a war of the colored races against the white. Hence England should have used every opportunity to head off what was plainly inevitable unless a way out could be found through mediation or wise counsel. But the Viceroy refused to confer with Gandhi after the Congress had voted its resolution, and the arrests followed, evidently in the belief that prompt and vigorous action and the use of unlimited force would nip the uprising in the bud.

Aida Pierce McCormick writes a circular letter from Arizona

Does England do to India the horrible things that Germany and Japan have done to captive countries?

No. She is much more humane. But if she now imprisons the intellectual and spiritual leaders of India; if she puts all of the Congress of India in prison and uses the lash on the common man who follows Gandhi, it will be hard for simple people, whether British or American, to remember how much worse the Nazis and Japanese are. It will confuse us. The dangers are a cynical disbelief in all the propaganda of freedom among our own people; also a deeper cynicism and despair among all our allies who are not white.

Many bodies and individuals have petitioned President Roosevelt but so far he has maintained silence except in commending the anniversary of the Atlantic Charter. Evidently Churchill knew what he was talking about when he said this Charter did not apply to India. The *Madras Hindu* says

Churchill has broken his own record by packing into a few hundred words more venom and more mischievous half truths than he treated the House of Commons to during the India bill debate in 1935. So far as India is concerned he is as dangerously irresponsible, as arrogantly contemptuous, as purblind as ever.

Prospect of a World Without Racial Conflict

It is with great regret that I do not see after this war, or within any reasonable time, the possibility of a world without race conflict; and this is true despite the fact that race conflict is playing a fatal role in the modern world. The supertragedy of this war is the treatment of the Jews in Germany. There has been nothing comparable to this in modern history. Yet its technique and its reasoning have been based upon a race philosophy similar to that which has dominated both Great Britain and the United States in relation to colored people.

This philosophy postulates a fundamental difference among the greater groups of people in the world, which makes it necessary that the superior peoples hold the inferior in check and rule them in accordance with the best interest of these superiors. Of course, many of the usual characteristics were missing in this outbreak of race hate in Germany. There was in reality little of physical difference between German and Jew. No one has been able to accuse the Jews of inferiority; rather it was the superiority of the Jews in certain respects which was the real cause of conflict. Nevertheless, the ideological basis of this attack was that of fundamental biological difference showing itself in spiritual and cultural incompatibility. Another difference distinguishes this race war. Usually the cure for race persecution and subordination has been thought to be segregation, but in this case the chance to segregate the Jews, at least partially, in Palestine, has practically been vetoed by the British government.

In other parts of the world the results of race conflict are clear. The representative of Prime Minister Churchill presiding over the

British war cabinet has been the prime minister of the Union of South Africa. Yet South Africa has without doubt the worst race problem of the modern world. The natives have been systematically deprived of their land, reduced to the status of a laboring class with the lowest of wages, disfranchised, living and working under caste conditions with only a modicum of education, and exposed to systematic public and private insult. There is a large population of mixed-bloods, and the poverty, disease, and crime throughout the Union of South Africa are appalling. Here in a land which furnishes gold and diamonds and copper, the insignia of the luxury and technique of modern civilization, this race hate has flourished and is flourishing. Smuts himself, as political leader of the Union of South Africa, has carried out much of the legislation upon which this race conflict is based; and, although from time to time he has expressed liberal ideas, he has not tried or succeeded in basically ameliorating the fundamental race war in that part of the world.

The situation in India is another case of racial conflict. The mass of people there are in the bondage of poverty, disenfranchisement and social caste. Despite eminent and widely known leadership, there has not come on the part of the British any effective attempt fundamentally to change the attitude of the governing country toward the subject peoples. The basic reason for this, openly or by inference, is the physical difference of race which makes it, according to British thought, impossible that these peoples should within any reasonable space of time become autonomous or self-governing. There have been promises, to be sure, from time to time, and promises are pending; but no one can doubt that if these people were white and of English descent, a way out of the present impasse would have long since been found.

There is no doubt but that India is a congery of ignorant, poverty-stricken, antagonistic groups who are destined to go through all the hell of internal strife before they emancipate themselves. But it is just as true that Europe of the sixteenth century was no more ready for freedom and autonomy than India. But Europe was not faced and coerced by a powerful overlord who did not believe Europeans were men and was determined to treat them as serfs to minister to his own comfort and luxury.

In India we have the first thoroughgoing case of modern colonial imperialism. With the capitalism built on the African slave trade and on the sugar, tobacco, and cotton crops of America, investment in India grew and spread for three hundred years, until there exists the greatest modern case of the exploitation of one people by another. This exploitation has been modified in various ways: some education has been furnished the Indians, a great system of railroads has been installed, and industrialism has been begun. But nothing has been done to loosen to any appreciable degree the stranglehold of the British Empire on the destinies of four hundred million human beings. The prestige and profit of the control of India have made it impossible for the British to conceive of India as an autonomous land.

The greatest and most dangerous race problem today is the problem of relations between Asia and Europe: the question as to how far "East is East and West is West" and of how long they are going to retain the relation of master and serf. There is in reality no difference between the reaction to this European idea on the parts of Japan and China. It is a question simply of the method of eliminating it. The idea of Japan was to invoke war and force—to drive Europe out of Asia and substitute the domination of a weak Asia by a strong Japan. The answer of China was cooperation and gradual understanding between Great Britain, France, America, and China.

Chinese leaders are under no illusions whatever as to the past attitude of Europe toward Chinese. The impudence, browbeating, robbery, rape, and insult is one long trail of blood and tears, from the Opium War to the kowtowing before the emperor in Berlin. Even in this present war and alliance, there has occurred little to reassure China: certain courtesies from the British and belated and meager justice on the part of the United States, after the Soong sister had swept in on us with her retinue, jade, and jewels. There has not only been silence concerning Hong Kong, Burma, and Singapore, but there is the continued assumption that the subjugation of Japan is in the interest of Europe and America and not of Asia. American military leaders have insisted that we must have in the Pacific after this war American bases for armed force. But why? If Asia is going to develop as a self-governing, autonomous part of the world, equal to other parts, why is policing by foreigners necessary? Why cannot Asia police itself? Only because of the deep-seated belief among Europeans and Americans that yellow people are the biological inferiors to the whites and not fit for self-government.

Not only does Western Europe believe that most of the rest of the world is biologically different, but it believes that in this difference lies congenital inferiority; that the black and brown and yellow people are not simply untrained in certain ways of doing and methods of civilization; that they are naturally inferior and inefficient; that they are a danger to civilization, as civilization is understood in Europe. This belief is so fundamental that it enters into the very reforms that we have in mind for the postwar world.

In the United States, the race problem is peculiarly important just now. We see today a combination of northern investors and southern Bourbons desiring not simply to overthrow the New Deal but to plunge the United States into a fatal reaction. The power of the southerners arises from the suppression of the Negro and poor-white vote, which gives the rotten borough of Mississippi four times the political power of Massachusetts and enables the South through the rule of seniority to pack the committees of Congress and to dominate it. Nothing can be done about this situation until we face fairly the question of color discrimination in the South; until the social, political, and economic equality of civilized men is recognized, despite race, color, and poverty.

In the Caribbean area, in Central and South America, European, African, there have been for four hundred years wide intermixture of

European, African, and Red Indian races. The result in one respect is widely different from that of Europe and North America; the social equality of Negroes, Indians, and mulattoes who were civilized was recognized without question. But the full results of this cultural liberalism were largely nullified by the economic control which Western Europe and North America held over these lands. The exploitation of cheap colored labor through poverty and low prices for materials was connived at as usual in the civilized world and the spoils shared with local white politicians. Economic and social prestige favored the whites and hindered the colored. A legend that the alleged backwardness of the South Americans was due to race mixture was so far stressed in the world that South America feared it and catered to it; it became the habit to send only white Brazilians, Bolivians, and Mexicans abroad to represent their countries; to encourage white immigration at all costs, even to loss of autonomy; to draw color lines in the management of industry dominated by Europe and in society where foreigners were entertained. In short, to pretend that South America hated and distrusted dark blood as much as the rest of the world, often even when the leaders of this policy were known themselves to be of Negro and Indian descent.

Thus the race problem of South and Central America, and especially of the islands of the Caribbean, became closely allied with European and North American practice. Only in the past few decades are there signs of an insurgent native culture, striking across the color line toward economic freedom, political self-rule, and more complete social equality between races.

There still is a residual sense of racial difference among parts of Europe; a certain contemptuous attitude toward Italy has been manifest for a long time, and the Balkans have been a byword for inefficiency and muddle. The pretensions of the Greeks to represent ancient Greek culture and of the Rumanians to be Roman have been laughed at by Western Europe. The remainder of the Balkans and Russia have been looked upon as Asiatic barbarism, aping civilization.

As quasi-Asiatic, they have come in for the racial contempt poured upon the yellow peoples. This attitude greeted the Russian Revolution and staged almost a race war to uphold tottering capitalism, built on racial contempt. But in Eastern Europe today are a mass of awakening men. They know and see what Russia has done for her debased masses in a single generation, cutting across race lines not only between Jew and Gentile but between White Russians, Ukrainians, Tartars, Turks, Kurds, and Kalmuks.

As Sidney and Beatrice Webb declared: "All sections of the community—apart from those legally deprived of citizenship on grounds unconnected with either race or nationality—enjoy, throughout the USSR, according to law, equal rights and duties, equal privileges and equal opportunities. Nor is this merely a formal equality under the law and the federal constitution. Nowhere in the world do habit and custom and public opinion approach nearer to a like equality in fact. Over the whole area between the Arctic Ocean and the Black Sea and the Central Asian mountains, containing vastly differing races and nationalities, men and women, irrespective of conformation of skull or pigmentation of skin, even including the occasional African Negro admitted from the United States, may associate freely with whom they please; travel in the same public vehicles and frequent the same restaurants and hotels; sit next to each other in the same colleges and places of amusement; marry wherever there is mutual liking; engage on equal terms in any craft or profession for which they are qualified; join the same churches or other societies; pay the same taxes and be elected or appointed to any office or position without exception." This, Eastern Europe knows, while Western Europe is still determined to build its culture on race discrimination and expects Russia to help her. But how far can Russia be depended upon to defend, in world war, British and American investments in Asia and Africa?

The attitude of America and Britain toward de Gaulle is puzzling until we remember that, since Gobineau, racial assumptions have entered into the relations between France and the Nordic world. During the First World War the United States was incensed at the social-equality attitudes of the "Frogs," while Britain as well as Germany resented the open dependence of France on her black colonial soldiers. One present great liberal statesman, Smuts, led a crusade against arming blacks in any future European war. Yet de Gaulle not only uses Senegalese soldiers but recognizes the Negro governor of a strategic French colonial province; while Burman writing of the history of the Free French, exclaims: "I am witnessing a miracle, the rebirth of France in the jungles of Africa!" Racial caste and profitable investment after the war indicate a halt in our support of de Gaulle. France since the eighteenth century has insisted on recognizing the social equality of civilized men despite race. She has for this reason been regarded as traitor to the white colonial front, in government and in society, despite her investors who have supported British methods. Hitler is not the only modern statesman who has sneered at "mongrel" France.

These are some, but by no means all, of the race problems which face the world; yet they are not being discussed except indirectly. The Atlantic Charter as well as the agreements in Moscow and Teheran have been practically silent on the subject of race. It is assumed that certain fundamental matters and more immediate issues must be met and settled before this difficult question of race can be faced. Let us now ask ourselves if this is true. What *are* the fundamental questions before the world at war?

If we measure the important matters by current discussion, we may range them somewhat as follows: (1) defense against aggression; (2) full employment after the war; (3) eventual fair distribution of both raw materials and manufactured goods; (4) abolition of poverty; and (5) health.

To anyone giving thought to these problems, it must be clear that each of them, with all of its own peculiar difficulties, tends to break asunder along the lesions of race difference and race hate. Among the primary factors entering into the discussion is the folklore and superstition which lurk in the minds of modern men and make them thoroughly believe, in accord with inherited prejudice and unconscious cerebration, that the peoples of the world are divided into fundamentally different groups with differences that are eternal and cannot be forgotten and cannot be removed. This philosophy says that the majority of the people of the world are impossible.

Therefore, when we discuss any of the listed problems, we usually see the solution within the frame of race and race difference. When we think of defense against aggression, we are thinking particularly of Europe, and the aggregation which we have in mind is not simply another Hitler but a vaster Japan, if not all Asia and the South Sea Islands. The "yellow peril" as envisaged by the German Emperor William II has by no means passed from the subconscious reactions of Western Europe. That is the meaning of the world police and "our way of life."

When we think of the problem of unemployment, we mean especially unemployment in the developed countries of Western Europe and America. We do not have in mind any fundamental change so far as the labor of the darker world is concerned. We do not think of full employment and a living wage for the East Indian, the Chinese coolie, and the Negro of South Africa or even the Negro of our own South. We want the white laborer in England and in America to receive a living wage and economic security without periodic unemployment. In such case we can depend on the political power of white labor to maintain the present industrial organization. But we have little or no thought of colored labor, because it is disfranchised and kept in serfdom by the power of our present governments.

This means, of course, that the industrial organization of these countries must be standardized; they must not clog their own avenues of trade by tariff restrictions and cartels. But these plans have very seldom gone far enough to envisage any change in the relations of Europe and America to the raw material of Africa and Asia or to accepting any idea of so raising the prices of this raw material and the wages of the laborers who produce it that this mass of labor will begin to approach the level of white labor. In fact, any such prospect the white laborers with votes in their hands would in vast majorities oppose.

In both the United States and the Union of South Africa it has been organized white laborers who have systematically, by vote and mob, opposed the training of the black worker and the provision of decent wages for him. In this respect, they have ranged themselves with exploiting investors and disseminators of race hatred like Hitler. When recently in the United States the President's Fair Employment Practices Commission sought to secure some steps of elementary justice for black railway workers, the railway unions refused even to attend the hearings. Only the Communists and some of the CIO unions have ignored the color line—a significant fact.

Our attitude toward poverty represents the constant lesion of race thinking. We have with difficulty reached a place in the modern white world where we can contemplate the abolition of poverty; where we can think of an industrial organization with no part of its essential co-operators deprived of income which will give them sufficient food and shelter, along with necessary education and some of the comforts of life. But this conception is confined almost entirely to the white race. Not only do we refuse to think of similar possibilities for the colored races but we are convinced that, even though it were possible, it would be a bad thing for the world. We must keep the Negroes, West Indians, and Indonesians poor. Otherwise they will get ambitious: they will seek strength and organization; they will demand to be treated as men, despite the fact that we know they are not men; and they will ask social equality for civilized human beings the world over.

There is a similar attitude with regard to health: we want white people to be well and strong, to "multiply and replenish the earth"; but we are interested in the health of colored people only insofar as it may threaten the health and wealth of whites. Thus in colonies where white men reside as masters, they segregate themselves in the most healthful parts of the country, provided with modern conveniences, and let the natives fester and die in the swamps and lowlands. It is for this reason that Englishmen and South Africans have seized the high land of Kenya and driven the most splendid of races of East Africa into the worst parts of the lowland, to the parts which are infested by the tsetse fly, where their cattle die, and they are forced laborers on white farms.

Perhaps in no area of modern civilized endeavor is the matter of race revealed more startlingly than in the question of education. We have doubts as to the policy of so educating the colored races that they will be able to take part in modern civilization. We are willing to educate them so that they can help in our industrial development, and we want them to become good workmen so long as they are unorganized. But when it comes to a question of real acquaintance-ship with what the more advanced part of the world has done and is doing, we try to keep the backward races as ignorant as possible. We limit their schools, their travel, and their knowledge of modern tongues.

There are, of course, notable exceptions: the Negro colleges of the southern United States, the Indian universities, and some advance even in university training in South Africa and in East and West Africa. But this advance is hindered by the fact that popular education is so backward that the number of persons who can qualify for higher training is very small, especially the number who can enter the professions necessary to protect the economic status of the natives and to guide the natives in avoidance of disease. In all these matters race interferes with education.

Beyond this we have only to mention religion. There is no denying that certain missionaries have done fine work in ameliorating the lot of backward people, but at the same time there is not a ghost of a doubt that today the organized Christian church is unfavorable toward race equality. It is split into racial sections and is not disposed to disturb to any great degree the attitude of civilization toward the Chinese, the Indians, and the Negroes. The recent pronouncement of the Federation of Churches of Christ was a fine and forward-looking document, but it has aroused no attention, much less enthusiasm, among the mass of Christians, and will not. The Catholic Church never champions the political or economic rights of subject peoples.

This insistent clinging to the older patterns of race thought has had extraordinary influence upon modern life. In the first place, it has for years held back the progress of the social sciences. The social sciences from the beginning were deliberately used as instruments to prove the inferiority of the majority of the people of the world, who were being used as slaves for the comfort and culture of the masters. The social sciences long looked upon this as one of their major duties. History declared that the Negro had no history. Biology exaggerated the physical differences among men. Economics even today cannot talk straight on colonial imperialism. Psychology has not yet recovered from the shame of its "intelligence" tests and its record of "conclusions" during the First World War.

Granted, therefore, that this is the basic attitude of the majority of civilized people, despite exceptions and individual differences, what must we expect after this war? In the first place, the British Empire is going to continue, if Mr. Churchill has his way, without "liquidation"; and there is slight chance that the English Labour Party or any other democratic elements in England are going to be able to get past the suspensory veto of the House of Lords and the overwhelming social power of the British aristocracy. In America the control of wealth over our democracy is going to be reinforced by the action of the oligarchic South. A war-weary nation is going to ignore reform and going to work to make money. If, of course, the greedy industrial machine breaks down in 1950 as it did in 1929, there will be trouble; but the Negroes will be its chief victims and sufferers.

Belgium has held its Congo empire with rare profit during the war, and the homeland will recoup its losses in Europe by more systematic rape of Africa. So Holland will batten down again upon the South Seas, unless the Japanese interlude forces some slight change of heart. South America will become an even more closely integrated part of British and American industry, and the West Indies will work cheaply or starve, while tourists throw them pennies.

The only large cause for disquiet on the part of Western Europe and North America is the case of Russia. There they are reassured as to the attitude of Stalin toward the working people of the Western world. Evidently he has decided that the Western European and American workers with votes in their hands are capable of deciding their own destiny; and, if they are not, it is their fault. But what is going to be the attitude of Russia toward colonial peoples? How far and where and when is Russia going to protect and restore British and American investments and control in Asia and Africa? Certainly her attitude toward the Chinese has shown in the past and still shows that she has the greatest sympathy with coolie labor and no love for Chiang Kai-shek. Will she have a similar attitude toward the other peoples of Asia, of Africa, and of the South Seas? If so, smooth restoration of colonial imperialism is not going to be easy.

What now can be done by intelligent men who are aware of the continuing danger of present racial attitudes in the world? We may appeal to two groups of men: first, to those leaders of white culture who are willing to take action, and second, to the leaders of races which are victims of present conditions. White leaders and thinkers have a duty to perform in making known the conclusions of science on the subject of biological race. It takes science long to percolate to the mass unless definite effort is made. Public health is still handicapped by superstitions long disproved by science; and race fiction is still taught in schools, in newspapers, and in novels. This careless ignorance of the facts of race is precisely the refuge where antisocial economic reaction flourishes.

We must then, first, have wide dissemination of truth. But this is not all: we need deliberate and organized action on the front where race fiction is being used to prolong economic inequality and injustice in the world. Here is a chance for a modern missionary movement, not in the interest of religious dogma, but to dissipate the economic illiteracy which clouds modern thought. Organized industry has today made the teaching of the elementary principles of economic thought almost impossible in our schools and rare in our colleges; by outlawing "communistic" propaganda, it has effectually in press and on platform almost stopped efforts at clear thinking on economic reform. Protest and revelation fall on deaf ears, because the public does not know the basic facts. We need a concerted and determined effort to make common knowledge of the facts of the distribution of property and income today among individuals; accurate details of the sources of income and conditions of production and distribution of goods and use of human services, in order that we may know who profits by investment in Asia and Africa as well as in America and Europe, and why and how they profit.

Next we need organized effort to release the colored laborer from the domination of the investor. This can best be accomplished by the organization of the labor of the world as consumers, replacing the producer attitude by knowledge of consumer needs. Here the victims of race prejudice can play their great role. They need no longer be confined to two paths: appeal to a white world ruled by investors in colored degradation, or war and revolt. There is a third path: the extrication of the poverty-stricken, ignorant laborer and consumer from his bondage by his own efforts as a worker and consumer, united to increase the price of his toil and reduce the cost of the necessities of life. This is being done here and there, but the news of it is suppressed, the difficulties of united action deliberately increased, and law and government united in colonial areas to prevent organization, manipulate prices, and stifle thought by force. Here colored leaders must act; but, before they act, they must know. Today, naturally, they are for the most part as economically illiterate as their masters. Thus Indian moneylenders are the willing instruments of European economic oppression in India; and many American and West Indian Negroes regard as economic progress the chance to share in the exploitation of their race by whites.

A union of economic liberals across the race line, with the object of driving exploiting investors from their hideout behind race discrimination, by freeing thought and action in colonial areas is the only realistic path to permanent peace today.

A great step toward this would be an international mandates commission with native representation, with power to investigate and report, and with jurisdiction over all areas where the natives have no effective voice in government.

Nehru

One of the most significant books of the war is the autobiography of Jawaharlal Nehru.[1] The book is significant not simply because, with great temperance and command of English, it tells the moving history of a life; but because both that life and the writing of the book are symbolic of the paradox and contradiction of the present world situation. Here is a man of Indian birth and Harrow and Cambridge education, who not only is writing his life in a British jail but has spent a large portion of his working days in such jails; and whose fault in the eyes of authority is exactly the object for which that same authority is fighting a world war, namely democracy; the firm determination of Nehru to achieve the autonomy and independence from the British Empire of the three hundred fifty million of India. As a peaceful, cultured and persistent advocate of this end he has not only been repeatedly imprisoned but lies in prison at this moment; has been beaten by the police on the street and seen friends killed and his mother beaten and sitting in her own blood; and must dedicate this volume to his wife, "Kamala Who Is No More," and who was driven to premature death by the struggle through which she and her husband had to pass. As the publisher says in his foreword, "Nehru is today the great democrat of the world. Not Churchill, not Roosevelt, not Chiang Kai-shek, in a sense not even Gandhi, stand as firm as Nehru does for government by the consent of the people and for the integrity of the individual."

Nehru was born in 1889 at Allahabad on the Ganges, in north central India. Sheltered as he was by well-to-do parents of the Brahmin caste, he nevertheless early sensed the shadow of the color veil. He knew that when an Englishman killed an Indian he was almost invariably acquitted by the jury; that on railway trains Europeans had reserved compartments while the Indians were crowded in their compartments like cattle. Benches and chairs were reserved for whites in public parks and when an Indian bested an Englishman the child was proud and glad. Yet he did not grow up to hate the English. On the whole, as he came to know them and was educated by English tutors and from the age of fifteen spent seven years in English schools, he conceived much admiration for the English. Yet he was also critical. With a predilection for a soft and easy existence and attracted a while by the gay life of London's West End, nevertheless he sympathized with the Boers in the Boer War and with the Japanese in the Russo-Japanese War and when in 1912, he returned to India for good, it was not indeed as a radical or a revolutionist but certainly as a friendly critic of England in India and as one who really know very little about the masses of the Indian people.

Then began his real education. Hew was swept into the unrest and protest then growing in India. He began to become acquainted with the crushing poverty of the masses, to meet them, to talk with them and live with them. He met Gandhi as early as 1916 and they became life long friends. He eventually joined the All India Congress movement, became a non-cooperator, helped in the boycott of the visiting Prince of Wales and refused to buy foreign cloth. He saw how his fellow Indians in the civil service became stool pigeons for the British. Especially he realized how Britain was crushing out freedom of thought and initiative: "It is estimated that above three hundred thousand persons have gone to prison at various times during the past fourteen years; and there can be no doubt that, politics apart, these three hundred thousand included some of the most dynamic and idealistic, the most socially minded and selfless people in India."

From a dilettante he became an earnest advocate of democracy for the masses. He began to believe in socialism and even in communism minus its violence. He played a larger and larger part in the wide Indian revolt; he joined the trades unions and so prominent did he become that it was proposed soon after the war began that he be made Premier of India "in fact if not in name" and the *New Statesman* of London added, "If we dare give India liberty we shall win the leadership of all free peoples. If we must meet a rebel India with coercion, will anyone in Europe or America mistake us for the champions of democracy?"

I must not deprive the reader of his own pleasure in following the struggles and disappointments of this extraordinary man, and especially of realizing the sweetness and balance of his temper. Few books of 450 pages have held me so enthralled. In comparison with the Negro problem in America one sees in Nehru's career astonishing resemblances: the violence, the stress upon religious submission, the inner difficulties within the Indian race and the way in which these difficulties have been played upon to the advantage of the English. The rather mysterious figure of Gandhi rises and take shape in this volume. Nehru loves Gandhi but does not fully agree with him, criticizes him sharply at various times but always defers to him and cooperates. From time to time during his fight to free India, Nehru visits Europe. He takes part in the Congress of Brussels which defends minorities. He visits Germany, Russia and Italy and then comes back to realize the insult of the Rowlett bills and the horrible massacre at Amritsar. One rises from the reading of this book with a feeling that the so-called race problems of the modern world are essentially one: primarily they are matters of economic exploitation, of racial arrogance and the utter failure to recognize in people of different color, appearance and ways of life, the essential humanity of all mankind.

Note

1. *Toward Freedom: The Autobiography of Jawaharlal Nehru*, The John Day Company, New York, 1941, 436 pp.

The Freeing of India

The fifteenth of August deserves to be remembered as the greatest historical date of the nineteenth and twentieth centuries. This is saying a great deal, when we remember that in the nineteenth century, Napoleon was overthrown, democracy established in England, Negro slaves emancipated in the United States, the German Empire founded, the partition of Africa determined upon, the Russian Revolution carried through, and two world wars fought. Nevertheless, it is true that the fifteenth of August marks an event of even greater significance than any of these; for on that date four hundred million colored folk of Asia were loosed from the domination of the white people of Europe.

It was not a gift nor act of grace. It was forced from the British Empire by the determination of the Indians themselves. Moreover, it was accomplished, not by blood and war, but by peace and grim determination. But for the action of one selfish man, M. A. Jinnah, originally encouraged by the English, there would have been practically no bloodshed in this vast revolution. Even as it is, the number of people killed in India by religious fanaticism during this emancipation is as nothing compared with the millions who fell in the American Civil War, in the Napoleonic Wars, and in two World Wars of Europe and America.

Indian Panorama

What is India? It is 1,500 thousand square miles of territory, with four hundred millions of people. They are mixed descendants of

Negroes and Negroids; Mongolians, Western Asiatics, and Eastern Europeans. They vary in color from black to white, and they are divided religiously into one hundred and fifty million Hindus, ninety million Mohammedans, thirteen million Sikhs, Jains and Christians, and many millions of smaller groups. They speak some two hundred and twenty-two languages and dialects.

The Indians are wretchedly poor. Lajpat Rai says: "The people of India are the poorest on earth. If there existed such poverty in any other country in Europe or America, the Government would have been turned out of office."

Sir William Hunter, one the most candid writers and a distinguished historian of India, Director-General of Indian statistics for many years, declared that 40 million of the people of India were seldom or never able to satisfy their hunger. It has been calculated that the average Indian family receives not more than twenty-five dollars a year. They are at least 75 percent illiterate and despite sixteen universities mostly of recent growth there are only fifteen million children in school. All this has been represented as taking place despite the philanthropy of Europe, and especially of England. This is of course a gross misinterpretation of history; it stems from the literary propaganda of which Rudyard Kipling was the especial example, which has led people for decades to picture India a great and backward country led by powerful, honest and semi-royal whites, and represented by a few gorgeously caparisoned Princes with millions of dollars in jewels and income.

Early Indian Education

Rev. F. E. Keay, writing on Ancient Indian Education, 1918, says that in the past Indian education was not inferior to the education of Europe, before the Revival of Learning. Not only did the Brahman educators develop a system of education which survived the crumbling of empires and the changes of society, but they also through all these thousands of years, kept aglow the torch of higher learning, and numbered amongst them many great thinkers who have left their mark not only upon the learning of India, but upon the intellectual life of the world.

When Buddhism came, it organized and developed a system of education. The Buddhist system was very much like the Brahmanical system from which it borrowed largely. Some of the Buddhist universities were of enormous size. Their high standards of learning attracted many scholars from China, some of whom have left on record description of these seats of learning. Buddhist education was by no means theological education. The study of medicine received special attention at the Buddhist universities. The Buddhist seats of learning did not shut their doors on any caste or creed. The high caste, the low caste, the Buddhist, the would-be Buddhist, the non-Buddhist, were all welcome. The contribution of Buddhist monks to elementary mass education was also considerable. Because of its Buddhist monasteries, practically every male adult in Burma was literate when the British set foot there.

The history of India is a story of change and tragedy. Three or four thousand years before Christ, a black people established civilization in the valley of the Ganges and other centers. Upon them descended invaders: Mongolians, from the east; Indo-Europeans from the west; and finally the great Mohammedan incursion in the sixteenth century and later. A fine and striking primitive civilization arose in India upon the black Dravidian foundation; it had a philosophy, a social organization, a splendid art.

In India was born, five centuries before Christ, one of the greatest of the world's religious leaders, usually depicted as black and crisp-haired, Gautama Buddha. He preached a religion of sacrifice and spiritual development. His religion spread over half the world. From 264 to 227 B.C. arose the great Emperor Asoka whose wheel is pictured on the new flag of Indian. He began a golden age which lasted a thousand years. After this era, when Indian civilization was one of the greatest in the world, with the Buddhist religion in the lead, there came a series of invasions; the Mongolian horde under Timur from the east; the Mohammedans from the west; invasions all fore-shadowed by the incursion of Alexander the Great 327 B.C.

In 1525, the great Moguls were reigning and the fame of their wealth and extravagance turned the attention of Europe toward India. From 1556 to 1605 reigned the great Emperor Ak-Bar and the Mohammedan empire glowed and died under his successors during the seventeenth century. By that time the attention of Europe was definitely turned toward India as a source of wealth, and in waves came the Portuguese, the Dutch, the French and finally the British. By the battle of Plassey in 1757 the English became masters of the fate of India. A great English writer Howitt tells of what the Dutch did in India:

> To secure dominion they compelled the princes of Ternate and Tidore to consent to the rooting up of all the clove and nutmeg trees in the island not entirely under the jealous safeguard of Dutch keeping. For this they utterly exterminated the inhabitants of Banda, because they would not submit passively to their yoke. Their lands were divided amongst the white people, who got slaves from other islands to cultivate them. For this Malacca was besieged, its territory ravaged, and its navigation interrupted by pirates; Negapatan was twice attacked; Cochin was engaged in resisting the kings of Calicut and Travancor, and Ceylon and Java were made scenes of perpetual disturbances. These notorious dissensions have been followed by as odious oppressions, which have been practiced at Japan, China, Cambodia, Arrácan on the banks of the Ganges, at Achen, Coromandel, Surat, in Persia, at Bassora, Mocha, and other places. For this they encouraged and established in Celebs a system of kidnapping the inhabitants for slaves which converted that island into a perfect hell.

English Repression

The record of the English was worse and longer:

> The power, the wealth, and the patronage brought home to them by the very violation of their own wishes and maxims were of such an

overwhelming and seducing nature that it was in vain to resist them. Nay, in such colours does the modern philosophy of conquest and diplomacy disguise the worst transactions between one state and another, that is it not for plain men very readily to penetrate to the naked enormity beneath.

But if there was ever one system more Machiavellian—more appropriative of the shew of justice where the basest injustice was attempted—more cold, more cruel, haughty, and unrelenting than another—it is the system by which the government of different states of India has been wrested from the hands of their respective princes and collected into the grasp of British power.

The condition of India before the Europeans came was favorable. The historian Feroz Shah (A.D. 1351–1394) expatiates on the happy state of the peasant, the goodness of their houses and furniture, and the general use of gold and silver ornaments by their women.

"The general state of the country must no doubt have been flourishing. Nicolo de Conti, who traveled about 1420 A.D., speaks highly of what he saw in Guzerat, and found the banks of the Ganges covered with towns amidst beautiful gardens and orchards, and passed four famous cities before he reached Maarazia, which he describes as a powerful city filled with gold, silver and precious stones. His accounts are corroborated by those of Barbora and Bartema, who traveled in the early part of the sixteenth century.

"Abdurizag, an ambassador from the grandson of Tamerlane, visited the South of India in 1442, and concurs with other observers in giving the impression of a prosperous country. The kingdom of Kandeish was at this time in a high state of prosperity under its own Kings; the numerous stone embankments by which the streams were rendered applicable to irrigation are equal to anything in India as works of industry and ability."

Baber speaks of Hindustan "as a rich and noble country and expresses his astonishment at the swarming population and the innumerable workmen of every kind and description." Political subjection to Europe followed in the nineteenth century.

Lajpat Rai, the great Indian martyr said:

Political subjection is the punishment of social evils and national crimes, but once imposed, it adds to their volume and intensity. It effectively checks any rejuvenation or reconstruction. It accentuates social evils and weaknesses. It leads to poverty in all its hideous forms, mental, moral and physical. If ever an awakening comes, it is delayed, or checked and crushed by all the forces of law and diplomacy, and of cunning and fraud. It is a part of the Imperial game to paint the subject people in the blackest colours, and to slander and libel them most shamelessly. The object is to produce and perpetuate the slave mentality of the subject people, and to obtain the moral sanction of the rest of the world for usurping the rights, properties, and liberties of other peoples. This is the genesis of the philosophy of the white man's burden. This is the mentality which stimulates the Empire-builder. This is the material with which the "steel frames" are forged to keep the subject peoples in hand and to prevent them from doing any harm to themselves, by aspiring to and working for their freedom. That is how Britain made her Empire in India.

Howitt says:

The first step in the English friendship with the native princes has generally been to assist them against their neighbours with troops, or to locate troops with them to protect them from aggression. For these services such enormous recompense was stipulated for, that the unwary princes, entrapped by their fears of their native foes rather than of their pretended friends, soon found that they were utterly unable to discharge them. Dreadful exactions were made of the subjects, but in vain. Whole provinces, or the revenues of them were soon obliged to be made over to their grasping friends but they did not suffice for their demands. In order to pay them their debts or their interest, the princes were obliged to borrow large sums at an extravagant rate. Theses sums were eagerly advanced by the English in their private and individual capacities, and securities again taken on lands or revenues. At every step the unhappy princes became more and more embarrassed, and as embarrassment increased, the claims of the company became proportionally pressing. In the technical phraseology of money-lenders the screw was then turned, till there was no longer any enduring it.

Indian Revolts

From the middle of the eighteenth century to the middle of the nine-teenth, bloody revolt and oppression was the history of this land. Revolts took place in 1758, 1775, 1782, 1790, 1805, 1814, 1817, 1823, 1837, 1844, 1850 culminating in the great mutiny of 1852. The stench of Indian misgovernment, graft, and theft at last made the British Crown take over the government from the celebrated East India Company. In 1858, India became a part of the British Empire, and in 1877 Victoria was made "Empress of India" by the great Jewish prime minister, Disraeli.

This did not stop, rather it began the inner struggle of India for freedom. Governors changed and became more liberal and cried to strive for better conditions in India; but the whole object of the British in India was still to make profit through private investment. And when the government interfered with investment, it simply meant that well-intentioned reform did not go through. The land became monopo-lized by money-lenders; industry became subservient to English trade; Indian art and artisanship was driven out of the market; the peasants and laborers became poorer and poorer and the whole country more and more ignorant. In spite of all the boasting of empire, England with her imperial might lay upon India like a blight.

The First World War brought matters to a crisis. Beginning in 1917 Great Britain tried to give India a constitution and rights, but arranged them on her own terms without allowing the Indians any voice in drawing up the new constitution. The great result of this effort was Mohandas Gandhi, the man who began his fight for free-dom in South Africa in behalf of both Indians and Negroes; and who now in India began his celebrated strife for peaceful rebellion, non-cooperation and self-rule in 1920.

The great Indian Congress was organized, one of the most success-ful voluntary organizations of peoples without rights that the world has ever seen. It stuck together in spite of differences in religion and aim and raised the cry of home rule in 1923. The British replied with elaborate shadow-boxing and propaganda. They called conferences in London, shot down protesters in India, and jailed the leaders, so that of the people now leading India there is not a single one who has not spent months and years in jail for demanding what they now have won in political and social freedom.

Finally because of the political results and economic complications of the Second World War, Great Britain had to let go; instead of India being in debt to Great Britain, Great Britain was hopelessly in debt to India, because of the raw materials which she had to draw from her during the war. The attitude of the Indian people was such that Great Britain did not dare compulsion. Some elements had even openly fought beside the Japanese. There was and is today wide interest in Russia and in Communism.

Divided India

Various gestures were made, the first brought by Cripps was rejected by the Indians; then the renegade Jinnah, a rich land-holder raised and pressed the religious question and succeeded in temporarily dividing India on the basis of Hinduism and Mohammedanism. Out of that, among the poor and ignorant, rose fanatical fighting among neighbors who had lived in peace for centuries. But the great Indian leaders were not to be diverted or misled. They decided wisely to accept freedom, even though it meant for the present a divided India. This division into Pakistan and the Union of India cannot stand, because Pakistan is an agricultural country, divided by the great triangle of India; unless then it can find support in Europe, which it cannot for long, it must depend upon India for industry which means that economic pressure will compel it to be one with the great subcontinent. So too the princely states will resist but succumb.

It is true that all will not go well with India. It is a difficult—a herculean task which this new nation undertakes. First of all, there are social problems; the education of a country which is vastly ignorant and needs all sort of education; there is the health problem among a people decimated by tropical disease, mal-nutrition and lack of clothing and shelter.

There is above all the problem of poverty; there is going to be increasingly a fierce struggle between the great Indian capitalists representing the tuition and the capital of Europe, and the mass of workers who have been ground down to the last degree of poverty and ill-health.

All of that drama of the rights of labor, which has been fought out in Europe and America, must be begun and struggled through in India. Then of course there is the problem of religion; age-old beliefs and superstitions, exacerbated by the Jinnah political program of throwing two great religions into difficult and bitter political competition. Nothing but an India-wide crusade against religious dogma will win here in the end. It must and will be undertaken.

Finally there is the whole problem of political power: the overall power of the state, the division of powers among the provinces; the question of votes and elections, and the various law-making bodies; all this portends for India a terrible and long struggle. But there is in this new land, certain great advantages. They have a spiritual faith; a belief in the inner value of the human being as different from and transcending the matter of wealth and material things. Indian philosophy and religion has influenced the world in this respect in the past; it will in the future. It may become dominant even over Europe, which measures everything in terms of profit.

American Negroes, particularly, have every reason to hail the new and free India. It is a freedom and autonomy of colored folk; it ends the day in a whole continent, when the white man by reason of the color of his skin, can lord it over colored people; when he can bring his segregation and his cheap habits of superiority, as shown by exclusive clubs, "jim-crow" cars and salaams and the other paraphernalia of disgraceful human degradation. The sun of the colored man has arisen in Asia as it will yet rise in Africa and America and the West Indies.

Gandhi and the American Negroes

Mohandas Gandhi was born nineteen months after my birth. As a school-boy in a small town in the north-eastern part of the United States, I knew little of Asia and the schools taught less. The one tenuous link which bound me to India was skin colour. That was important in America and even in my town, although little was said about it. But I was conscious of being the only brown face in my school and although my dark family had lived in this valley for two hundred years or more, I was early cognizant of a status different from that of my white school-mates.

As I grew up there seemed to be no future for me in the place of my birth, and at seventeen I went South, where formerly coloured people had been slaves, so that I could be trained to work among them. There at Fisk University I first became aware of a world of coloured folk and I learned not only of the condition of American Negroes but began to read of China and India; and to make Africa the special object of my study. I published my first book in 1896 while Gandhi was in South Africa, and my subject was the African slave trade. We did not at the time have much direct news from Africa in the American newspapers, but I did have several black students from South Africa and began to sense the tragedy of that awful land. It was not until after the First World War that I came to realize Gandhi's work for Africa and the world.

I was torn by the problem of peace. As a youth I was certain that freedom for the coloured peoples of the earth would come on by war; by doing to white Europe and America what they had done to black Africa and coloured Asia. This seemed the natural conclusion from the fairy tales called history on which I had been nourished. Then in the last decades of the nineteenth century, as I came to manhood, I caught the vision of world peace and signed the pledge never to take part in war.

With the First World War came my first knowledge of Gandhi. I came to know Lajpat Rai and Madame Naidu. John Haynes Holmes was one of my co-workers in the National Association for the Advancement of Coloured People, and he was a friend and admirer of Gandhi. Indeed the "Coloured People" referred to in our name was not originally confined to America. I remember the discussion we had on inviting Gandhi to visit America and how we were forced to conclude that this land was not civilized enough to receive a coloured man as an honoured guest.

In 1929, as the Depression loomed, I asked Gandhi for a message to American Negroes, which I published in the *Crisis*. He said: "Let not the 12 million Negroes be ashamed of the fact that they are the grandchildren of slaves. There is dishonour in being slave-owner. But let us not think of honour or dishonour in connection with the past. Let us realize that the future is with those who would be pure, truthful and loving. For as the old wise men have said: Truth ever is, untruth never was. Love alone binds and truth and love accrue only to the truly humble."

This was written on May day, 1929. Through what phantasmagoria of hurt and evil the world has passed since then! We American Negroes have reeled and staggered from side to side and forward and back. In the First World War, we joined with America capital to keep Germany and Italy from sharing the spoils of colonial Imperialism. In the Depression we sank beneath the burden of poverty, ignorance and disease due to discrimination, unemployment and crime. In the Second World War, we again joined Western capital against Fascism and failed to realize how the Soviet Union sacrificed her blood and savings to save the world.

But we did realize how out of war began to arise a new coloured world free from the control of Europe and America. We began too to realize the role of Gandhi and to evaluate his work as a guide for the black people of the United States. As an integral part of this country, as workers, consumers and co-creators of its culture, we could not look forward to physical separation except as a change of masters. But what of Gandhi's program of peace and non-violence? Only in the last year have American Negroes begun to see the possibility of this program being applied to the Negro problems in the United States.

Personally I was long puzzled. After the World Depression, I sensed a recurring contradiction. I saw Gandhi's non-violence gain freedom for India, only to be followed by violence in all the world. I realized that the vaunted "hundred years of peace," from Waterloo to the Battle of the Marne, was not peace at all but war, of Europe and North America on Africa and Asia, with only troubled bits of peace between the colonial conquerors. I saw Britain, France, Belgium and North America trying to continue to force the world to serve them by monopoly of land, technique and machines, backed by physical force which has now culminated in the use of atomic power. Only the possession of this power by the Soviet Union prevents the restoration of colonial imperialism of the West over Asia and Africa, under the leadership of men like Dulles and Eden. Perhaps in this extraordinary impasse the teachings of Mahatma Gandhi may have a chance to prevail in the world. Recent events in the former slave territory of the United States throw a curious light on this possibility.

In Montgomery, Alabama, the former capital of the Confederate States which fought for years to make America a slave nation, the black workers last year refused any longer to use the public buses on which their seats had long been segregated from those of the white passengers, paying the same fare. In addition to separation, there was abuse and insult by the white conductors. This custom had continued for seventy-five years. Then last year a coloured seamstress got tired of insult and refused to give her seat to a white man. Black workers led by young, educated ministers began a strike which stopped the discrimination, aroused the state and the nation and presented an unbending front of non-violence to the murderous mob which hitherto has ruled the South. The occurrence was extraordinary. It was not based on any first-hand knowledge of Gandhi and his work. Their leaders like Martin Luther King knew of non-resistance in India; many of the educated teachers, business and professional men had heard of Gandhi. But the rise and spread of this movement was due to the truth of its underlying principles and not to direct teaching or propaganda. In this aspect it is a most interesting proof of the truth of the Gandhian philosophy.

The American Negro is not yet free. He is still discriminated against, oppressed and exploited. The recent court decisions in his favour are excellent but are as yet only partially enforced. It may well be that the enforcement of these laws and real human equality and brotherhood in the United States will come only under leadership of another Gandhi.

The Colonial Groups
in the Postwar World

In the lectures which I am planning to deliver in Haiti, I want to examine with you the prospective status of the colonial groups in the world after the conclusion of this war and in the organization of peace for the future. You will I am sure bear with my imperfect French in this intricate and difficult task.

First of all I am deliberately using the word "colonial" in a much broader sense than is usually given it. A colony, strictly speaking, is a country which belongs to another country, forms a part of the mother country's industrial organization, and exercises such powers of government, and such civic and cultural freedom, as the dominant country allows. But beyond this narrower definition, there are manifestly groups of people, countries and nations, which while not colonies in the strict sense of the word, yet so approach the colonial status as to merit the designation semicolonial. The classic example of this status has long been China. There are other groups, like the Negroes of the United States, who do not form a separate nation and yet who resemble in their economic and political condition a distinctly colonial status. It was a governor of the state of Georgia [Ellis G. Arnall] who said in the recent Democratic nominating convention in Chicago: "We cannot continue as a nation to treat thirteen millions of our citizens as semi-colonials." Then, too, there are a number of nations whose political independence is undisputed and who have a certain cultural unity; and yet by reason of their economic ties with the great industrial and capital-exporting countries, find themselves severely limited in their freedom of action and opportunity for cultural development. They are in a sense the economic colonies of the owners of a closely knit world of global industry. The Balkan countries and those of South and Central America, and the Caribbean area occupy in varying degrees this sort of semi-colonial status.

Looking therefore upon this colonial and semicolonial world, I wish first to ask what common characteristics we may discern; how these characteristics exhibit themselves in the different groups, and how these groups suffer common disabilities and hindrances with social classes in the more advanced lands of the world; and finally, what place these colonies should and will occupy in the democracy which we hope will gradually inherit the earth.

There are in the first place certain characteristics of colonial peoples, which are so common and obvious that we seldom discuss them and often actually forget them; colonial and quasi-colonial peoples are as a mass, poverty-stricken, with the lowest standards of living; they are for the most part illiterate and unacquainted with the systematized knowledge of modern science; and they have little or no voice in their own government, with a consequent lack of freedom of development. Naturally these characteristics vary widely among different groups and nations; so that before we generalize, make comparisons and seek remedies, we must stop to examine certain specific types of colonial countries. This examination, I shall make in very general terms in this lecture. Later I hope to treat in more detail various selected lands.

Let us first consider the colonies proper: the countries of America, Africa and Asia which we usually designate as colonies. In America, we have the British West Indies, the French islands, the American acquisitions. All of these conform to a well-known type: at the top, a group of varying size, consisting mainly of whites and mulattoes; they are in income, often well-to-do and sometimes rich; they are literate and in some cases highly cultured, and they have some voice in government. Below this group, and composing from 75 to 90 percent, are a mass of people, predominantly of direct African descent, illiterate largely, and making a decent living with difficulty; subject to disease, with high infant mortality, and having for the most part no voice in government, and with restricted personal freedom.

Discussion of this situation in the past and largely today, confines itself to the persisting disabilities of the elite, to questions of their political power and cultural recognition. There can be no question but that these matters are of grave concern and call for remedy. But our preoccupation with these problems which in so many cases are peculiarly personal, must no longer blind us to the much vaster problem: as to how far it is necessary that in the most beautiful part of the New World, the overwhelming mass of the inhabitants be precluded by poverty, ignorance, disease and disfranchisement from taking any effective part in modern civilization. White citizens of the United States and most Englishmen find nothing unusual or alarming in this situation. They have argued from the days of the slave trade that not more than a tenth of the Caribbean peoples are capable of modern civilization or conceivable participants in political and cultural democracy. Without any profound dissent, many of the colored folk themselves have accepted this dictum without question and confined their protest against social conditions to the situation of the elite, which certainly and justly demands betterment.

But how has it been decided, and who has decided, that the social distribution of the Caribbean is normal and inevitable? We are led to question the conclusion all the more, when we remember that it is not long since when the overwhelming proportion of the populations of most European countries was as poor and ignorant as modern colonial peoples. In answer to this reflection, the nineteenth century posed the question of "Race," of the existence of such inborn and ineradicable difference between stocks of human beings as made the proportion of civilizable people vastly different in Europe and America, and between the lighter and darker folk. I need not remind you how fierce a controversy arose over this theory of race, and how that pseudo-science long hindered not simply remedy for the degradation of colonials, but even conception of the possibility of remedy. Today as we stand near halfway through a century which has proven the biological theories of unchangeable race differences manifestly false, what difference of action does this call for on our part?

First of all it calls our attention to the fact that so far as science is concerned, there is no earthly reason why the elite of Haiti, Jamaica, Martinique and Cuba should not comprise nine-tenths instead of one-tenth of the population. If this be true, what hinders steps toward its realization? Such steps must begin with knowledge; with concerted effort such as I am indicating in this lecture, to study colonial and quasi-colonial status in various parts of the world. Turning to the colonies of Africa, we find certain differences and contrasts with the West Indies. In the colonies of West Africa and East Africa, the emerging group of the elite as a recognizable class is largely missing. There are outstanding personalities, and social movements, but instead of conforming to the European class pattern, they link themselves to another and a different social heritage. The tradition of a strong and ancient organization persists—an organization that linked the mass of the people directly to the chief through an intricate nobility; in this society the tribe became an integral state in which the interests of no individual were neglected.

There has recently been published a most thoroughgoing study of the Kingdom of Nupe in Nigeria. Any person, white or black, who has a lingering conception that Africa evolved no political state, should read this book. But in this case as in most African colonies, there has cut across this ancient pattern, changing, spoiling and even partially obliterating it, the modern colonial system, born in the West Indies and transferred to the source of the developed slave trade. This system substitutes for the local, home-born and home-developed elite, foreign control, represented by a mere handful of more or less temporary representatives, who govern the tribe or state. The objects of this government determine the character of the colony. The earlier African colonies were for purposes of trade, and all government was directed toward facilitating trade. Outside that, the colony conducted its own affairs in its own way.

Then certain valuable articles of trade came into greater demand and pressure was brought to bear to increase the supply. Slave trade and slavery resulted overseas, but on the African mainland, gold, vegetable oils, copper and diamonds, became more valuable than slaves in the West Indies, and the tribal organization was partially or wholly disrupted to supply regular labor. The value of these new products undermined the foundations of slavery in the new world. Slavery, therefore, disappeared from the New World especially when Toussaint and others used force to accelerate this development. On the other hand, the African colony became therefore a vast business organization to reap profit for European investors out of the invested capital and forced labor of Africa. Across this cut the efforts of missionaries and philanthropists and West Indian and American Free Negroes. The result today is a series of African colonies, conducted for profit, and yet with their policy modified so as to recognize in varying degree the development and progress of the native. With all the advance made, it is fair to say that the investment motive is still supreme in West and East Africa. It is less powerful in French Senegal, but in the Belgian Congo, while changed materially from the disgraces of Leopold, it is still an investment far more than a philanthropy. In South Africa, strong tribal organization met modern industrial exploitation and finance capital, head-on. The result is the most complicated race problem on earth, with retrogression and reaction fighting against almost every forward movement of the native proletariat and opposed by a small but growing philanthropy on the part of the whites.

Turning now to Asia, we face the problem of India, the largest colony in the world and the one that poses the greatest colonial problem. In India we have an ancient culture, an intricate political history, and a long economic development. On this fell the power of the West and East: the East with organized military power; the West, first with the religious might of organized Mohammedanism meeting the spiritual seeds of indigenous Buddhism. On this was thrown in the century before the widest growth of the African slave trade, the newly organized power of the new capitalism, which American slavery had given birth to in England. The loot of India by European political adventurers and merchants established modern capitalism in Europe and with the accompanying technical and scientific inventions, gave Europe mastery of the world. Capitalism was a great and beneficent method of satisfying human wants, without which the world would have lingered on the edge of starvation. But like all invention, the results depend upon how it is used and for whose benefit. Capitalism has benefited mankind, but not in equal proportions. It has enormously raised the standard of living in Europe and even more in North America. But in the parts of the world where human toil and natural resources have made the greatest contribution to the accumulation of wealth, such parts of the earth, curiously enough, have benefited least from the new commerce and industry. This is shown by the plight of Africa and India today. To be sure Africans and Indians have benefited by modern capital. In education, limited though it be; in curbing of disease, slow and incomplete as it is; in the beginning of the use of machines and labor technique; and in the spread of law and order, both Negroes and Hindus have greatly benefited; but as compared with what might have been done; and what in justice and right should have been accomplished, the result is not only pitiful, but so wrong and dangerous as already to have helped cause two of the most destructive wars in human history, and is today threatening further human death and disaster.

To realize this, look at India today. No one has ever tried to prove that its vast horde of three hundred and fifty million people are not normal human beings and as gifted as the Europeans. No one denies that Indians have worked hard and long, have been cunning in technique, profound in thought and lofty in religious ideal. Yet this land after three hundred years' subjection to European political control and industrial domination, is poverty-stricken to an inconceivable degree, is 90 percent illiterate, is diseased and famine-cursed, and has limited voice in its own government. It is for instance in this war not by its own consent but by declaration of Great Britain. Thousands of its leaders who have dared peacefully to protest against this situation are today in jail.

Dutch and French India approach, with some modifications and variations, the British Indian pattern; in other words, India, while a partner in the development of modern capitalistic civilization, and while sharing some of its benefits, has received so small and inadequate a share as compared with Europe that its present plight is a disgrace to the world. And this is because the modern world under the guidance of Europe and North America has become used to thinking that the plight of the human millions of Asia and Africa is normal, essentially right and unchangeable except after long periods of evolution if even then.

Let us now turn to certain states which are not colonies but which for various reasons approximate the colonial status. Some of these are China, many of the countries of South America and groups like the Negroes in the United States and the Indians of the Americas. To these may be added the majority of the Balkan states, the states of the Near East, and the independent Negro countries, Liberia, Haiti and Ethiopia. In these cases there is recognized political independence, and a cultural heritage of varying strength and persistence. But on the other hand in all these cases, the economic dependence of the country on European and North American industrial organization, in commerce, in sale of raw materials and especially in obtaining the use of capital in the shape of machinery and manufactured material—this dependence on world industry makes the country largely dependent on financial interests and cultural ideals quite outside the land itself. There have been many cases where this partnership between a land of labor and material, and a land of wealth, technical efficiency and accumulated capital goods, has worked advantageously for both. But in most modern instances, the wealthy country is thinking in terms of profit, and is obsessed with the long-ingrained conviction that the needs of the weaker country are few and its capacity for development narrow or nonexistent. In that case, this economic partnership works to the distinct disadvantage of the weaker country. The terms of sale for raw materials, the prices of goods and rent of capital; even the wages of labor are dictated by the stronger partner, backed by economic pressure and military power.

The case of China is well known. The seat of the oldest civilization surviving in the world, China was compelled at gunpoint to trade with Europe. This procedure was justified as leading to the Christianization and economic uplift of this great land. The results justified this method only in part. For the most part the colonial pattern prevailed: a mass of poverty-stricken people, illiterate and diseased, with their political autonomy partially nullified; until when native resentment revolted in the late nineteenth century, Europe planned to divide the country into colonies. This was delayed by the rise of Japan as a major power and her insistence on sharing the spoils. From this point the path to World War was straight and clear.

The Indian and Negro group in America have paused on a threshold, leading by one door to complete integration with the countries where they reside; and by another door leading to the organization of a sort of nation within a nation, which approaches colonial status on the one hand and eventual incorporation on the other. The Indians have taken one path, and the Negroes of the United States the other. The eventual result is not clear, and depends to a degree on the development of the colonial status among other peoples of the world. In the case of the Balkans and the Near East, a strong cultural tradition, urges them toward independent nationhood, while the elite of their own people, especially the great landlords, the new manufacturers and home capitalists, stand in such close alliance with and dependence on the European industrial and financial organization, that most of these countries remain bound hand and foot by a web of their own weaving. This is peculiarly true of Poland, Hungary, Bulgaria and Rumania. In South America, the pattern changes, because the cultural heritage and bond is weaker, and the social conditions in Europe become guide and ideal for the independent American colony. The normal situation, with poverty, ignorance, disease and disfranchisement seems in the eternal nature of things and nearly all effective effort is expended on raising an elite which shall be recognized by Europe and share the privileges of Europeans. Only in comparatively recent days, has an ideal arisen in lands like Chile, Peru and Brazil, of a spiritually independent South America, with a people of white, red and black blood intermingled, and with a laboring class as high in standards of living and political rights as the best of European lands.

The independent Negro nations, Haiti, Liberia and Ethiopia, suffer first from the widespread assumption of the nineteenth century, that Africa and the black race were not an integral part of the human picture and consequently could not and must not be allowed to try to develop like other nations along the lines of economic uplift, social development and political independence. We Negroes who in the last half century have convinced ourselves of our equality with mankind and our ability to share modern culture, scarcely realize how high a wall of prejudice based on color we have still to surmount today. This makes us all the more eager to force recognition of our worth, and too often forgetful of how the burden rests on us as on all peoples, to increase and increase rapidly and widely among the masses of people within our group who are still depressed in poverty, ignorance, and disease, and incapable of adding to the total of the emerged classes, the ability, physical strength and spiritual wealth, of which they are possessed. The studied and bitter attack on Liberia because of alleged slave raiding was of minor importance so far as the facts were concerned. Britain, France, Spain, Belgium and other countries had been pursuing and still were pursuing in some cases in Africa identical methods of labor recruitment as Liberia.

But beyond the bare facts was the allegation that Liberia was using against her own people the methods which she protested when used by whites. Even this was not really true, but it had enough semblance of truth, to hurt Liberia deeply. The same tactics used against Ethiopia almost fixed the charge of slavery upon this land at the very time she was making hard effort to abolish the slave status. I need not remind you how often and persistently the charge of voodooism brought against you has so twisted the clear truth as to emphasize the denial of cultural equality to a land which has in so many instances led America in cultural development. Yet here the truth is that your culture elite, with all its fine accomplishments, is not anywhere near as large as wealth, education and health might raise from your peasantry.

Now let me sum up this preliminary survey of the colonial problem: the depressed peoples and classes of the world form the vast majority of mankind today in the era of the highest civilization the world has known. The majority of human beings do not today have enough to eat and wear or sufficient shelter for decent existence; the majority of the world's peoples do not understand what the world is, what it has been and what the laws of its growth and development are; and they are unable to read the record of this history. Most human beings suffer and die years before this is necessary and most babies die before they ever really live. And the human mind with all its visions and possibilities is today deliberately distorted and denied freedom of development by people who actually imagine that such freedom would endanger civilization. Most of these disinherited folk are colored, not because there is any essential significance in skin color, but because most people in the world are colored.

What now can be done about this, in this day of crisis, when with the end of a horrible and disgraceful war in sight, we contemplate Peace and Democracy? What has Democracy to do with Colonies and what has skin-color to do with Peace?

PART IV

The East Is Red

Revolutions and Resolutions

The most veiled and contentious aspect of Du Bois's career is without question his support for Communism. Du Bois's decision to join the Communist Party of the United States in 1963, encouraged by his wife Shirley Graham, a member before he was, culminated more than seventy years of support for the ideals of socialism. Yet most significantly for this book, Du Bois's choice to turn Communist pledged specific allegiance to the leadership of Maoist China and other Asian independence struggles which, to Du Bois's mind, gave the world the most advanced working model of what a colored people's revolution could be. Du Bois's lifelong consternation over allegiance to Marxism was colored steadily by two perceptions: that Marxism was primarily a Eurocentric body of thought best suited to describing the exploitation of white European workers, not colored workers; that white supremacy remained a consistent part of Marxist, socialist and labor movements in the western European and North American world.

The year 1949 struck an illuminating blow against both of these conceptions. The formation of China's People's Republic coincided with Du Bois's deep alienation from and disaffection with capitalist reformism and liberal democracy as well as a re-energized optimism about the potentiality of anticolonial movements. Maoism split this difference for Du Bois. It was, to paraphrase Aimè Césaire, an example of "Marxism in the service of colored people rather than colored people in the service of Marxism." China's example also synthesized several recurring ideals in Du Boisian thought: that communalism and collectivism, in part indebted to African social organizing ideals, ought to structure human society; that a viable political alternative to Cold War polarities of U.S. and Soviet was necessary and important to the future of African Americans; that the primary aim of a successful Third World movement would necessarily be the defeat of capitalist imperialism. Too, China's 1949 revolution was perceived by Du Bois, as by most black U.S. radical intellectuals of the 1950s and 1960s, as a turning point in the relationships of First to Third World, and a clarion call to build alliances in the Afro-Asian world. This was the import of the 1955 Bandung Conference, which we have seen remained a touchstone for Du Bois long after its conclusion.

This final section of *Crossing the World Color Line* samples some of the transformative writings of Du Bois's last and final phase. "The East Is Red: Revolutions and Resolutions" selects work from 1950 to 1961. The section opens with several short but symbolically important selections from Du Bois's "As the Crow Flies" columns from the *Chicago Globe*. Du Bois began writing for the *Globe* after he was summarily dismissed from his position as columnist for the *Chicago Defender* for his openly radical views in 1948. In 1950, former *Defender* editor Metz Lochard started the *Globe*, a progressive weekly, and invited Du Bois to become a columnist there. Du Bois's columns appeared in the *Globe* from April to December of 1950.

"As the Crow Flies" had been the title of Du Bois's column for the *Crisis* until its discontinuation in the 1930s. The first three selections here are from manuscripts for the column produced by Du Bois between August 9 and August 23, 1950. They are individually attuned to conditions in Indonesia, Burma, and Malaysia (or here, Malaya) respectively. The columns are dispatches from the spreading anticolonial front intended to build interest and support among Du Bois's American readers in the potential rise of a Pan-Asian revolution against racism and colonialism. The essays are strategically scaled to this effect. Du Bois recuperates elements of the racialism evident in his writings on antiquity by reminding black readers at home that "The people of Malaya are yellow Mongolians grafted on Negroes; Negroes who were the greatest sailors of the ancient world and Mongolians who represented the great empires of China." As in *The World and Africa*, though, Du Bois's racial historiography is in the purpose of building a fighting spirit that can cross the world color line. Likewise, in his column on Indonesia, Du Bois celebrates the formation of the Indonesian Republic in 1949 but cautions that "The colonial regime is doomed, but it is not gone." Indonesia, as its history has aptly shown, had miles to go Du Bois felt before it could claim itself free from the economic, racial, and social subordination of colonialism.

The next selection is a fascinating retrospective on war and peace and Du Bois's final commentary on the legacy of Mahatma Gandhi. "Will the Great Gandhi Live Again?" was published in the progressive weekly newspaper *National Guardian* in honor of Negro History Week, February 11, 1957. Du Bois was an irregular contributor to the *Guardian* throughout the 1950s. As in his earlier essays, Du Bois uses the life and work Gandhi as a yardstick of his own shifting positions on the contradictions of war. The essay is, politically and philosophically, a muddle: it perceives the "paradox of peace and war" as a failure of human sympathy and understanding, on one hand, yet an outgrowth of a systematic violence against African Americans rooted in slavery and the Civil War. The essay is fueled by Du Bois's frustration and the increasing intensity of both national war-mongering in the U.S. and the concomitant violence of southern white supremacy. Du Bois is sympathetic to King's efforts to bring nonviolent resistance to U.S. civil rights struggle, but is skeptical about its capacity to reverse centuries of "pathological" Western and U.S. hatred of blacks.

The essay is ultimately a demonstration of why Du Bois moved further after 1957 into a historical materialist analysis of race and capitalism whose dialectical method provided a means for addressing precisely what Du Bois calls here the "contradiction and riddle" of American racism.

The final three selections comprise a late trilogy of Du Bois's writings on China and China's Communist revolution. The first, "Our Visit to China," was first published in the magazine *China Pictorial* on March 20, 1959. The essay, written near the end of a four-month visit Du Bois and Shirley took to the Soviet Union and China, is an almost wistful account of a dream deferred. Du Bois explains, "Visits like this, on our own and on the part of all Americans, ought to have been made during the last twenty-five years." However, Cold War restrictions on travel—an indirect reference to the stripping of his own passport in 1952—have for American citizens "not only limited . . . their right to travel, but . . . the right to learn the truth about the Revolution which is sweeping the world." Shirley and he have come to China, he writes, "to learn the facts in this crisis of modern civilization." What Du Bois discerns is a people who suffered even more than black Americans—"I know that no depths of Negro slavery in American have plumbed such abysses as the Chinese have for two thousand years and more"—and yet have marshaled one of the world's most profoundly successful revolutions. The essay provides a flattering and uncritical history of China's march toward freedom. It is an intoxicating return of good will to a nation that opened its political and diplomatic arms at a time when Du Bois was feeling more un-American than ever.

The book concludes with two essays featuring Du Bois in a mood of revolutionary sublime. "The Vast Miracle of China Today," published in the *National Guardian* June 8, 1959, is a breathless and sweeping travelogue of China's Communist successes, a kind of social realistic landscape painting in words. It includes positive commentary on the role of women and abolition, as Du Bois perceives it, of sexism and gender difference, but is in the main a manifesto for the elimination of class and race prejudice under Communism. Du Bois contends that despite its problems China has successfully "exorcised the Great Fear that haunts the West; the fear of losing his job; the fear of falling sick; the fear of accident; the fear of inability to education his children." The essay is also significant for what it doesn't include. Du Bois's tours of China were tightly controlled by the State to foreground the successes of the Revolution. Economic problems, agricultural underdevelopment, food shortages, and political repressions attendant to China's revolutionary policies of the 1950s were either ignored by Du Bois or kept from his field of vision. These omissions continue to contribute to criticism of Du Bois's support for China. They also be speak the level of disappointment Du Bois had registered for western democracy, and the continuing faith he had in collective action and dialectical struggle to achieve long-term liberation for people of color.

The book concludes with perhaps Du Bois's single most euphoric essay on the possibility of both Asian liberation and the long-sought alliance between the black and yellow worlds. "China and Africa" was written as a speech delivered by Du Bois on February 22, 1959, on the occasion of a national celebration of his ninety-first birthday in Beijing. The speech was delivered to more than one thousand students and faculty at Peking University and broadcast on national radio. The essay is a utopian love letter from Du Bois to China, asking her to turn her revolutionary face to Africa so that the two might join hands. Likewise, the essay appeals to both the Africans possibly present in Peking as part of international exchange agreements, and the Africans decolonizing at home, to recognize China as the true spiritual and political leader of the colored world. The essay is tactile and visceral, an anatomy of racial romanticism and revolutionary fervor. "China is flesh of your flesh and blood of your blood," Du Bois writes to his black brothers around the world. "China is colored and knows to what a colored skin in this modern world subjects its owner. But China knows more, much more than this: she knows what to do about it." The essay closes with an improvised moment of archetypal recasting: it is the "Hebrew prophet of Communism" who beckons to the black and Asian worlds the dream of a promised land "without money and without price." The essay serves as Du Bois's final farewell to China. It also serves as an epitaph and exclamation point to Du Bois's lifelong wish to solve the "riddle" of Asia.

Publication History for Part IV

"Indonesia." Manuscript for "As the Crow Flies" column, *Chicago Globe*, 1950.

"Burma." Manuscript for "As the Crow Flies" column, *Chicago Globe*, 1950.

"Malaya." Manuscript for "As the Crow Flies" column, *Chicago Globe*, 1950.

"Will the Great Gandhi Live Again?" *National Guardian* (Feb. 11): 1957.

"Our Visit to China." *China Pictorial*, n. 6 (March 20, 1959): pp. 4–5.

"The Vast Miracle of China Today." *National Guardian* (June 8, 1959).

"China and Africa." First published in *Peking Review*, V. 2 (March 3, 1959): pp. 11–13; also in *New World Review* (April 1, 1959): pp. 28–31; and in *The World and Africa*. New York: International Publishers, 1972, pp. 311–17.

Indonesia

Once I was walking along the streets of the Hague in Holland. I was a young student on my way to Germany and I wanted to see everything and know all about it. I wanted direction to some place, I forget which, and seeing a man near me I asked him. He was an officer in uniform; he looked at me and stiffened a bit, and before giving me any directions he said slowly, in carefully mustered English: "Do you not usually raise your hat when you address an officer?" I told him, "No, I do not." I might have explained that in my country at that time we did not hold officers in particularly high esteem; certainly we did not regard them as rulers of the universe. We were looking forward to a continued era of peace. All this I did not explain, but after I had gotten my directions, I raised my hat and thanked the pompous ass courteously. I became aware that here I had run across another of those peculiar problems of the "color line." This plain sleek little Holland owned several millions of colored peoples overseas, and expected from them deference and service. It was the first time that I became aware of Indonesia.

Isles of the Eastern Seas

Stretched across the waters from Asia to Australia, between the Indian Ocean and the Pacific and occupying a space as large as that of the original thirteen states, live 75 million colored people on a network of islands from the huge Sumatra through narrow Java to great Borneo and Celebes. North are the Philippines, geographically a part of this

175

group; and south is the vast waste of waters down the South Pole. These are colored people, and deeply colored. They range from yellow to dark brown, carrying in their veins the blood of Africa and Asia, and forming a great and ancient center of history and civilization.

I remember once coming in contact with a significant aspect of that civilization. I had been invited to speak in London and certain patriotic American women objected to my presence at the leading London Women's Club. It was then that Her Highness Ranee of Sarawak took me under her patronage and as [wife of the reigning Rajah] had me publically to dinner and brought a most distinguished audience to listen to my speech with its arraignment of the color line in the United States and the British Empire. Now Sarawak is a bit of Borneo which an English official had given to him with the native title, and which the British Empire with malice aforethought continued to recognize until quite recently.

Japan and Indonesia

In the future we will recognize that the Japanese did not attack the white West in vain. It all came so suddenly and quickly and then was so quickly wiped out by the Second World War that today we are like to forget it. But remember that a great yellow nation rose up and drove Europe out of Asia in a short time and with miraculous thoroughness, and thereafter Asia did not return docile to the protection of Europe, particularly in Indonesia. These brown people led by Sockarne helped drive the Japanese out, but then objected to the Dutch returning. Thereupon rose war between the Dutch and her colonies. That war from 1947 to 1949 was the effort of the colonies to make the Dutch recognize and put into action a long series of vague promises of autonomy. The East Indians demanded freedom and demanded it now.

Why was it Holland wanted to hold these islands? It was of course the old story, the islands raised rice, coffee, rubber and quinine; they made Holland rich and clean and gleaming; they made life in Holland comfortable; they supplied Holland and the world with bulbs of beautiful tulips. But the colonies starved.

Indonesian Art

All that we of the West heard of these East Indies for decades was their art. They and we were drugged by it. Man cannot live without beauty. He has to have song, dance and ornaments; and this the traveler saw in Java and the other islands of the Eastern Indies; but they did not realize that while people need expression of beauty, they must also eat. The peoples of Indonesia like the peoples of Asia, were continually starving. They had schools, but schools for the few. They had some educated men who went to Holland for their training. They had families of mixed white and colored folk and these mulattoes too often became leaders who kept the mass of the darker folk down. All this began to pall after the needling which Japan thrust into the arms of these people. There came revolt and self assertion and finally in 1949, there came the recognition of the Indonesian Republic.

The Republic of Indonesia

So today we have a great nation of brown people, new to the world and struggling with new and intricate problems. These problems are the world old problems of how they may eat and drink and be sheltered and yet not be slaves to their work and slaves to other folk who get riches from their work. The colonial regime is doomed, but it is not gone. Indonesia is trying to take over the control of her industry, trying to let Dutch capital remain but not rule, trying to assert domination of New Guinea which is yet being withheld, trying to have the recognition of the peoples of the world for its independence. It has not accomplished this yet, but it is on its way.

Burma

Rice

In my New England home, no meal was complete without potatoes. They were called "Irish Potatoes," and they became an integral part of our food because of Irish immigrants. In Ireland potatoes could grow when little else could and poor peasants lived almost wholly on them; without the potatoes there was no life. So when the potato famine came in 1845 the Irish in droves migrated to America and brought us the potato habit, although perhaps we had some of it before. As potatoes are in New England, so rice is to the South, and especially to Asia and the islands of the seas. So that when one thinks of life among the larger part of human beings, they think of rice. And Burma has often been called the "rice bowl" of Asia, because of the 12 million acres given to its cultivation and its quality in the estimation of the peoples round about.

Burma

Burma is a country of 17 million people, descendants of original Negroids upon whom the Mongolians of the North descended. It has a tropical climate with a rainy season and a dry season and occupies one of the many great river valleys running north and south which makes the sub-continent of India. It raises rice and teak-wood, tin and petroleum. Its rubies, sapphires, and jade are unsurpassed in beauty and quality.

The history of Burma is part of the history of India. The East India company began the subjugation of Burma in the early seventeenth century, then afterward, Great Britain systematically subdued the country. In 1823 and for three years she managed to beat the Burmese army and make the country pay a large tribute. In 1852, the Burmese were attacked again and their country annexed. In 1885 came the third Burmese war caused by taxation on a rich British trading company. The king was overthrown and the whole country annexed.

Separate Burma

Meantime, the Burma Oil Company was founded in 1871, by a Scotch merchant. From small beginnings it expanded until in 1928 it had a capital of $50,000,000 and was producing annually 800,000 tons of oil. This company, in association with the iron and steel works of India, made a tremendous and exceptional center of exploitation. The British thought it well to divide and conquer. Therefore in 1922, Burma was cut off from India and set up as a separate colony under British control. This was looked upon as a thoughtful method of keeping the whole sub-continent in control. Burma was given wider franchise and took part in the First World War. But after the Second World War, Goshal tells us what the British did:

"The government of the United Kingdom advanced a loan of £87 million to Burma, to finance a series of 'Projects' under the direction of the Civil Supplies Board. These 'Projects' were assigned only to British firms, such as Steel Bros., Imperial Tobacco Co., Lever Bros. etc. The Inland Water Transport Project was assigned to the Irrawaddy Flotill Company under rather startling financial arrangements.

"What all this really amounted to was that the government employed the assets of these companies, provided a large part of new capital necessary, guaranteed the companies' profits, protected them from competition, and, through its control over wages, insured a supply of cheap labor.

"The government guaranteed compensation to British firms for war losses, but made no such provision for the Burmese people whose lands had been destroyed, nor for the families of guerilla fighters who had given their lives in the war. Despite the fact that the rice crop for 1945–46 was 2,700,000 tons as against a normal crop of 7,000,000 tons and that the supply of draft animals had been reduced to half the pre-war number, the government made no request for UNRRA aid. By the beginning of 1947, only rudimentary steps had been taken to aid the peasants of Burma, who constitute the overwhelming majority of the population."

Nevertheless when the crisis came and India gained her independence, Burma became independent too. Today it occupies 250,000 square miles or an area equal to France, Belgium and Holland. It is a republic and became completely independent outside the British Commonwealth by a Treaty which became effective in 1948. It is the fifty-eighth member of the United Nations.

But the Burmese are not satisfied. It is a little difficult to know all the details about the basis of their dissatisfaction, but it depends as everywhere in Asia upon the economic situation. The Karens, a people forming less than a tenth of the population have pressed for autonomy; but beyond this, a large number of the Burmese want better control of industry, better division of land and a higher standard of living. So that the country has been rocked with civil war and dissension, since 1948. Many Europeans hope fervently that this civil war will lead to the re-conquest of Burma under British dominion or American influence, but so far they have been disappointed and there is no reason to think that Burma is going to disappear from the new community of nations into the colonial status.

Malaya

Not all American Negroes have the thrill which I had when I heard of the fall of Singapore to Japanese arms. I knew that the world had passed a milestone. Singapore was the magnificent playground, brothel and whore-house for the white man in the East. As Kipling remarked jauntily: "There were no ten commandments" in Singapore. The white man was master of the yellow and the world about him. It was a magnificent city of a million people. Eighty steamship lines sent thirty thousand ships a year. There were great banks, modern office buildings and stately government palaces. There were prostitutes and gambling halls; liquor and gold flowed like water. It was a fine place for the rich white masters of the world to play.

The Malay States

The Malay States are not large as compared with Indonesia. They have been gotten together by every kind of theft and lie of which the British Empire was capable. There were the Federated Malay states with only 37 thousand square miles and two million people; there were the Unfederated states of about the same size and population. There was the States Settlements with a million people; and there was Singapore. In addition to this there was rubber, tin, rice and pepper, camphor and palm oil. But above all the Malay states were trading grounds. Here everything from East to West met and was exchanged; and here in the exchange, men and nations made millions. Until after

World War II. Then the people of the Malay states determined to take charge of their own country, and Great Britain having lost India and having politically lost Burma and having had to give up to America the lucrative trading rights of the world, was determined to keep this trading post. She is fighting there today, and cannot send troops to Korea because too many of her troops are dying in the jungles of Malaya. She is determined to keep Malaya and Malaya is determined not to be kept.

The Last of Colonialism

It is often said that colonial imperialism is at an end in this world. We would better say that the end is in sight; or rather in the vision of certain men. It has not yet really ended. There is great and bitter determination on the part of Europe and investors in America, to keep certain colonial outposts, in order to make profits and dominate at least part of the world. Remember what the essence of colonialism is: it is the high point of efficiency reached by capitalism. In a single country with the eyes of the people upon the employers and manu-facturers, there are distinct and growing limits as to what these owners of industry may do. In most civilized countries they cannot today depress the wages below a certain floor; they must make arrangements with their employees, with their unions, and on the conditions of work and wages; they face strikes and public sympathy when they try to drive their workers below a certain standard of living.

On the contrary, there are no such limitations, when the workers, instead of being in one's own country and before the eyes of public opinion, are across wide seas; have no political rights and little edu-cation; and have no way by which they can put their situation before the home country.

The people who are experts upon their condition are employees of the employers and they say what they are told to say or they lose their jobs. Consequently conditions in colonies according to colonial officials are always bright; the colony is always advancing and so long as the profits keep up, the colony loves to be under the domination of the home country! The one great objection to this rosy picture, is that when we really learn of the situation of the colonies, it is absolutely contradicted. In every colony, the people are wretchedly poor and diseased, so that colonial regions are the sick poverty stricken regions of the world. In every country there is determined effort to see that the colonists have no real educated leadership. It is this that makes the colonial question, still the burning question of the world; and in no place is the fight for freedom stronger and with greater excuse than in Malaya today.

The People of Malaya

The people of Malaya are yellow Mongolians grafted on Negroes; Negroes who were the greatest sailors of the ancient world and Mongolians who represented the great empires of China. In the sixteenth century the castigation and degradation of the Malayian people began when the Portuguese occupied Malacca and began to seek cloves and nutmegs. For the next ten years the Portuguese explored and occupied the Archipelago. Then came Spain under Magellan. War and anarchy followed and finally came the English and the Dutch in the sixteenth century. Gradually the islands of Malaya and India were divided between the Dutch and English and the Portuguese nearly crowded out. The English centered their trade at Malaya, the Dutch in Sumatra and Java. Malaya became early the distributing center of spices on route from India to Europe. Soon the English by treaty and by seizure, by negotiation and by cheating became the paramount power in Malaya with puppet Sultans under their sway. Now the people have begun to fight for freedom.

Will the Great Gandhi Live Again?

The greatest philosopher of our era pointed out the inherent contradictions in many of our universal beliefs; and he sought eventual rec-
onciliation of these paradoxes. We realize this today. Our newly
inaugurated President asks the largest expenditure for war in human
history made by a nation, and proclaims this as a step toward peace!
We have larger endowments devoted to peace activity than any other
nation on earth, and less activity for abolishing war.

As I look back on my own attitude toward war during the last
seventy years, I see repeated contradiction. In my youth, nourished
as I was on fairy tales, including some called History, I quite naturally
regarded war as a necessary step toward progress. I believed that if my
people ever gained freedom and equality, it would be by killing white
people.

Then, as a young man in the great afflatus of the late nineteenth
century, I came to believe in peace. No more war. I signed the current
pledge never to take part in war. Yet during the First World War, "the
war to stop war," I was swept into the national maelstrom.

After the depression I sensed recurring contradictions. I saw Gandhi's
non-violence gain freedom for India, only to be followed by violence in
all the world; I realized that the hundred years of peace from Waterloo
to 1914 was not peace at all, but war of Europe on Africa and Asia, with
troubled peace only between the colonial conquerors. I saw Britain,
France, and America trying to continue to force the world to serve them
by using their monopoly of land, technique, and machinery, backed by
gunpowder, and then threatening atomic power.

Then Montgomery in Alabama tried to show the world the synthesis of this antithesis. And not the white Montgomery of the Slave Power; not even the black Montgomery of the Negro professional men, merchants, and teachers; but the black workers: the scrubbers and cleaners; the porters and seamstresses. They turned to a struggle not for great principles and noble truths, but just asked to be let alone after a tiring day's work; to be free of petty insult after hard and humble toil. These folk, led by a man who had read Hegel, knew of Karl Marx, and had followed Mohandas Karamchand Gandhi, preached: "Not by Might, nor by Power, but by My Spirit," saith the Lord. Did this doctrine and practice of non-violence bring solution of the race problem in Alabama? It did not. Black workers, many if not all, are still walking to work, and it is possible any day that their leader will be killed by hoodlums perfectly well known to the white police and the city administration, egged on by white councils of war, while most white people of the city say nothing and do nothing.

All over the lower South this situation prevails. Despite law, in the face of drooling religion and unctuous prayer, while the nation dances and yells and prepares to fight for peace and freedom, there is race war, jails full of the innocent, and ten times more money spent for mass murder than for education of children. Where are we, then, and whither are we going? What is the synthesis of this paradox of eternal and world-wide war and the coming of the Prince of Peace?

It lies, I think, not in the method but in the people concerned. Among normal human beings, with the education customary today in most civilized nations, non-violence is the answer to the temptation to force. When threat is met by fist; when blow follows blow, violence becomes customary. But no normal human being of trained intelligence is going to fight the man who will not fight back. In such cases, peace begins and grows just because it is. But suppose they are wild beasts or wild men? To yield to the rush of the tiger is death, nothing less. The wildness of beasts is nature; but the wildness of men is neglect and, often, our personal neglect. This is the reason beneath our present paradox of peace and war.

For now near a century this nation has trained the South in lies, hate, and murder. We are emphasizing today that when Robert E. Lee swore to serve the nation and then broke his word to serve his clan, his social class, and his private property—that this made him a hero; that although he did not believe in human slavery, he fought four long years, with consummate skill, over thousands of dead bodies, to make it legal for the South to continue to hold four million black folk as chattel bondsmen—that this makes him a great American and candidate for the Hall of Fame.

We have for eighty years as a nation widely refused to regard the killing of a Negro in the South as murder, or the violation of a black girl as rape. We have let white folk steal millions of black folks' hard-earned wages, and openly defended this as natural for a "superior" race. As a result of this, we have today in the South millions of persons who are pathological cases. They cannot be reasoned with in matters of race. They are not normal and cannot be treated as normal. They are ignorant and their schools are poor because they cannot afford a double school system and would rather themselves remain ignorant than let Negroes learn.

Remedy for this abnormal situation would be education for all children and education all together, so as to let them grow up knowing each other as human. Precisely this path these abnormal regions refuse to follow. Here, then, is no possible synthesis. So long as a people insults, murders and hates by hereditary teaching, non-violence can bring no peace. It will bring migration until that fails, and then attempts at bloody revenge. It will spread war and murder. Can we then by effort make the average white person in states like South Carolina, Georgia, Alabama, Mississippi, and Louisiana normal, intelligent human beings?

If we can, we solve our antithesis; great Gandhi lives again. If we cannot civilize the South, or will not even try, we continue in contradiction and riddle.

Our Visit to China

I am an American in the sense that I was born in the United States where my forebears have lived for two centuries. We have worked and voted there, paid taxes and served in the armed forces. We have made some contribution to American culture. On the other hand, I am in the fifth generation, an African. In the eighteenth century, a Dutch trader seized my great-great grandfather on the coast of West Africa, transported him to New Amsterdam which is now the state of New York, and sold him as a slave. He gained his freedom by fighting in the American Revolution to free America from Great Britain. The great-great-granddaughter of this Tom Burghardt married the great-grandson of a French Huguenot, who had migrated to America in the seventeenth century and some of whose descendants had gone to the West Indies to avoid fighting England. One of these had a mulatto concubine and his grandson married my mother. I am their son, hence my French name. My wife Shirley Graham was also born in America, of African and Scotch-Irish decent; and her grandfather was a Cheyenne Indian. Few persons have better right to call themselves American.

Nevertheless our people for three hundred years have had to struggle for recognition as American citizens, because most of our folk were in slavery or worked as low-paid serfs for exploiting whites. Many whites joined us in our struggle, and thus our people have gained important victories in our fight for equality in the last two centuries. This battle still goes on and must be continued until Negroes are recognized as equal to other American citizens.

Why did such a conflict ever arise? It was because of the greed of mankind. Because despite the abundance of a rich new continent, slave labour was found to provide a few persons with wealth and power created by this exploited labour. When the nobler souls of America, conceived this continent as the home of a new democracy where workers would share the wealth which they created with their fellows on equal terms, they were faced by the contradiction of Negro slavery. For eighty-seven years after they had declared "All men are born equal," this nation refused to abolish slavery. Then came Civil War, not to abolish slavery but to stop its expansion to parts of the nation where the workers were free. This could be not be accomplished until the slaves helped the freesoilers at the price of their freedom. This they secured in 1863.

But even since then, the nation, instead of giving the black slaves full freedom, tried to turn them into a colour caste of serfs, and this is the so-called Negro Problem of the United States today. Negroes have progressed in their fight for equality, but their battle is not yet won. The cause is that when the African slave trade ceased, there arose Colonial Imperialism which sought to reduce most of the world's workers to serfs of Western Europe and North America, and to build civilization on their exploited labour. To this scheme the rising socialism of the Soviet Union and China is a fatal threat; but this fact the mass of American Negroes do not yet realize. To be able to tell them the truth about Communism, I and my wife have been in the Soviet Union and China for four months, and intend to stay until May Day. Here I have spent my ninety-first birthday. And here we have met sympathy and welcome for which we are deeply thankful.

Visits like this, on our own part and on the part of all Americans ought to have been made during the last twenty-five years. Indeed I visited the Soviet Union in 1926, 1936 and 1949. I had a brief glance at China in 1936. But just when knowledge of the rise of Socialism would have been most valuable, the "Cold War" started and for ten years American citizens have been not only limited in their right to travel, but even in the right to learn the truth about the Revolution which is sweeping the world. Fantastic tales of the failure of Socialism and the impossibility of Communism fill our periodicals and books. Most Americans today are convinced that Socialism has failed or will fail in the near future. But not all Americans and few Europeans believe this. The threat of war today is because so much of the world is convinced that private capitalism is doomed and fighting its last failing battle with a past based on human degradation for most people in the world. We are here to learn the facts in this crisis of modern civilization.

The Vast Miracle of China Today

A Report on a Ten-Week Visit to the People's Republic of China

I have traveled widely on this earth since my first trip to Europe sixty-seven years ago. Save South America and India, I have seen most of the civilized world and much of its backward regions. Many leading nations I have visited repeatedly. But I have never seen a nation which so amazed and touched me as China in 1959 .

I have seen more impressive buildings but no more pleasing architecture; I have seen greater display of wealth, and more massive power; I have seen better equipped railways and boats and vastly more showy automobiles; but I have never seen a nation where human nature was so abreast of scientific knowledge; where daily life of everyday people was so outstripping mechanical power and love of life so triumphing over human greed and envy and selfishness as I see in China today.

It is not a matter of mere numbers and size; of wealth and power; of beauty and style. It is a sense of human nature free of its most hurtful and terrible meannesses and of a people full of joy and faith and marching on in a unison unexampled in Holland, Belgium, Britain and France; and simply inconceivable in the United States.

A typical, ignorant American put it this way in Moscow: "But how do you make it go without niggers?" In China he would have said: "But see them work": dragging, hauling, lifting, pulling—and yet smiling at each other, greeting neighbors who ride by in autos, helping strangers even if they are "niggers"; seeking knowledge, following leaders and believing in themselves and certain destiny. Whence comes

190

this miracle of human nature, which I never saw before or believed possible?

I was ten weeks in China. There they celebrated my ninety-first birthday with a thoughtfulness and sincerity that would simply be impossible in America even among my own colored people. Ministers of state were there, writers and artists, actors and professional men; singers and children playing fairy tales. Anna Louise Strong came looking happy, busy and secure. There was a whole table of other Americans, exiled for daring to visit China; integrated for their skills and loyalty.

I have traveled 5,000 miles, by railway, boat, plane and auto. I saw all the great cities: Peking, Shanghai, Hankow and its sisters; Canton, Chungking, Chengtu, Kunming and Nanking. I rode its vast rivers tearing through mighty gorges; passed through its villages and sat in its communes. I visited its schools and colleges, lectured and broadcast to the world. I visited its minority groups. I was on the borders of Tibet when the revolt occurred. I spent four hours with Mao Tse-tung and dined twice with Chou En-lai, the tireless Prime Minister of this nation of 680 million souls.

The people of the land I saw: the workers, the factory hands, the farmers and laborers, scrubwomen and servants. I went to theaters and restaurants, sat in the homes of the high and the low; and always I saw happy people; people with faith that needs no church nor priest and laughs gaily when the Monkey King fools the hosts of Heaven and overthrows the angels.

In all my wandering, I never felt the touch or breath of insult or even dislike—I who for ninety years in America scarcely ever saw a day without some expression of hate for "niggers."

What is the secret of China in the second half of the twentieth century? It is that the vast majority of a billion human beings have been convinced that human nature in some of its darkest recesses can be changed, if change is necessary. China knows, as no other people know, to what depths human meanness can go. I used to weep for

American Negroes, as I saw through what indignities and repressions and cruelties they had passed; but as I have read Chinese history in these last months and had it explained to me stripped of Anglo-Saxon lies, I know that no depths of Negro slavery have plumbed such abysses as the Chinese have seen for 2,000 years and more. They have seen starvation and murder: rape and prostitution; sale and slavery of children; and religion cloaked in opium and gin, for converting the "Heathen." This oppression and contempt came not only from Tartars, Mongolians, British, French, Germans and Americans, but from Chinese themselves: Mandarins and warlords, capitalists and murdering thieves like Chiang Kai-shek; Kuomintang socialists and intellectuals educated abroad.

Despite all this, China lives, and has been transformed and marches on. She is not ignored by the United States. She ignores the United States and leaps forward. What did it? What furnished the motive power and how was it applied?

First it was the belief in himself and in his people by a man like Sun Yat-sen. He plunged on, blind and unaided, repulsed by Britain and America, but welcomed by Russia. Then efforts toward socialism, which wobbled forward, erred and lost, and at last was bribed by America and Britain and betrayed by Chiang Kai-shek, with its leaders murdered and its aims misunderstood, when not deliberately lied about.

Then came the Long March from feudalism, past capitalism and socialism to communism in our day. Mao Tse-tung, Chou En-lai, Chu Teh and a half dozen others undertook to lead a nation by example, by starving and fighting; by infinite patience and above all by making a nation believe that the people and not merely the elite— the workers in factory, street, and field—composed the real nation. Others have said this often, but no nation has tried it like the Soviet Union and China.

And the staggering and bitter effort of the Soviets, beleaguered by all Western civilization, and yet far-seeing enough to help weaker

China even before a still weak Russia was safe—on this vast pyramid has arisen the saving nation of this stumbling, murdering, hating world.

In China the people—the laboring people, the people who in most lands are the doormats on which the reigning thieves and murdering rulers walk, leading their painted and jeweled prostitutes—the people walk and boast. These people of the slums and gutters and kitchens are the Chinese nation today. This the Chinese believe and on this belief they toil and sweat and cheer.

They believe this and for the last ten years their belief has been strengthened until today they follow their leaders because these leaders have never deceived them. Their officials are incorruptible, their merchants are honest, their artisans are reliable, their workers who dig and haul and lift do an honest day's work and even work overtime if the state asks it, for they are the State; they are China.

A kindergarten, meeting in the once Forbidden City, was shown the magnificence of this palace and told: "Your fathers built this, but now it is yours; preserve it." And then pointing across the Ten An Men square to the vast building of the new Halls of Assembly, the speaker added: "Your fathers are building new palaces for you; enjoy them and guard them for yourselves and your children. They belong to you!"

China has no rank nor classes; her universities grant no degrees; her government awards no medals. She has no blue book of "society." But she has leaders of learning and genius, scientists of renown, artisans of skill and millions who know and believe this and follow where these men lead. This is the joy of this nation, its high belief and its unfaltering hope.

China is no Utopia. Fifth Avenue has better shops where the rich can buy and the whores parade. Detroit has more and better cars. The best American housing outstrips the Chinese and Chinese women are not nearly as well-dressed as the guests of the Waldorf-Astoria. But the Chinese worker is happy.

He has exorcised the Great Fear that haunts the West; the fear of losing his job; the fear of falling sick; the fear of accident; the fear of inability to educate his children; the fear daring to take a vacation. To guard against such catastrophe Americans skimp and save, cheat and steal, gamble and arm for murder.

The Soviet citizen, the Czech, the Pole, the Hungarian have kicked out the stooges of America and the hoodlums set to exploit the peasants. They and the East Germans no longer fear these disasters; and above all the Chinese sit high above these fears and laugh with joy.

They will not be rich in old age. They will not enjoy sickness but they will be healed. They will not starve as thousands of Chinese did only a generation ago. They fear neither flood nor epidemic. They do not even fear war, as Mao Tse-tung told me. War for China is a "Paper Tiger." China can defend itself and back of China stands the unassailable might of the Soviet Union.

Envy and class hate is disappearing in China. Does your neighbor have better pay and higher position than you? He has this because of greater ability or better education, and more education is open to you and compulsory for your children.

The young married couple do not fear children. The mother has prenatal care. Her wage and job are safe. Nursery and kindergarten take care of the child and it is welcome, not to pampered luxury but to good food, constant medical care and education for his highest ability.

All this is not yet perfect. Here and there it fails, falls short and falters; but it is so often and so widely true, that China believes, lives on realized hope, follows its leaders and sings:

"O, Mourner, get up offa your knees." The women of China are free. They wear pants so that they can walk, climb and dig; and climb and dig they do. They are not dressed simply for sex indulgence and beauty parades. They occupy positions from ministers of state to locomotive engineers, lawyers, doctors, clerks and laborers. They are escaping household "drudgery"; they are strong and healthy and beautiful not simply of leg and false bosom but of real brain and brawn.

In Wuhan, I stood in one of the greatest steelworks of the world. A crane which moved a hundred tons loomed above. I said, "My God, Shirley, look up there!" Alone in the engine-room sat a girl with ribboned braids, running the vast machine.

You won't believe this, because you never saw anything like it; and if the State Department has its way, you never will. Let *Life* lie about communes; and the State Department shed crocodile tears over ancestral tombs. Let Hong Kong wire its lies abroad. Let "Divine Slavery" persist in Tibet until China kills it. The truth is there and I saw it.

America makes or can make no article that China is not either making or can make better and cheaper. I saw its export exposition in Canton: a whole building of watches, radios, electric apparatus, cloth in silk and wool and cotton; embroidery, pottery, dishes, shoes, telephone sets. There were five floors of goods, which the world needs and is buying in increasing quantities, except the ostrich United States, whose ships rot.

Fifteen times I have crossed the Atlantic and once the Pacific. I have seen the world. But never so vast and glorious a miracle as China.

China and Africa

By courtesy of the government of the 680 million people of the Chinese Republic, I am permitted on my ninety-first birthday to speak to the people of China and Africa and through them to the world. Hail, then, and farewell, dwelling places of the yellow and black races. Hail human kind!

I speak with no authority: no assumption of age nor rank; I hold no position, I have no wealth. One thing alone I own and that is my own soul. Ownership of that I have even while in my own country for near a century I have been nothing but a "nigger." On this basis and this alone I dare speak, I dare advise.

China after long centuries has arisen to her feet and leapt forward. Africa arise, and stand straight, speak and think! Act! Turn from the West and your slavery and humiliation for the last five hundred years and face the rising sun. Behold a people, the most populous nation on this ancient earth which has burst its shackles, not by boasting and strutting, not by lying about its history and its conquests, but by patience and long-suffering, by hard, backbreaking labor and with bowed head and blind struggle, moved up and on toward the crimson sky. She aims to "make men holy; to make men free." But what men? Not simply the mandarins but including mandarins; not simply the rich, but not excluding the rich. Not simply the learned, but led by knowledge to the end that no man shall be poor, nor sick, nor ignorant; but that the humblest worker as well as the sons of emperors shall be fed and taught and healed and that there emerge on earth a single unified people, free, well and educated.

196

You have been told, my Africa: My Africa in Africa and all your children's children overseas; you have been told and the telling so beaten into you by rods and whips, that you believe it yourselves, that this is impossible; that mankind can only rise by walking on men, by cheating them and killing them; that only on a doormat of the despised and dying, the dead and rotten, can a British aristocracy, a French cultural élite or an American millionaire be nurtured and grown. This is a lie. It is an ancient lie spread by church and state, spread by priest and historian, and believed in by fools and cowards, as well as by the downtrodden and the children of despair.

Speak, China, and tell your truth to Africa and the world. What people have been despised as you have? Who more than you have been rejected of men? Recall when lordly Britishers threw the rickshaw money on the ground to avoid touching a filthy hand. Forget not the time when in Shanghai no "Chinaman" dared set foot in a park which he paid for. Tell this to Africa, for today Africa stands on new feet, with new eyesight, with new brains and asks: Where am I and why? The Western sirens answer; Britain wheedles; France cajoles; while America, my America, where my ancestors and descendants for eight generations have lived and toiled, America loudest of all, yells and promises freedom. If only Africa allows American investment. Beware Africa, America bargains for your soul. America would have you believe that they freed your grandchildren; that Afro-Americans are full American citizens, treated like equals, paid fair wages as workers, promoted for desert and free to learn and earn and travel across the world. This is not true. Some are near freedom, some approach equality with whites, some have achieved education; but the price for this has too often been slavery of mind, distortion of truth and oppression of our own people. Of 18 million Afro-Americans, 12 million are still second-class citizens of the United States, serfs in farming, low-paid laborers in industry, and repressed members of labor unions. Most American Negroes do not vote. Even the rising six million are liable to insult and discrimination at any time.

But this, Africa, relates to your descendants, not to you. Once I thought of you Africans as children, whom we educated Afro-Americans would lead to liberty. I was wrong. We could not even lead ourselves, much less you. Today I see you rising under your own leadership, guided by your own brains.

Africa does not ask alms from China nor from the Soviet Union nor from France, Britain, nor the United States. It asks friendship and sympathy and no nation better than China can offer this to the Dark Continent. Let it be given freely and generously. Let Chinese visit Africa, send their scientists there and their artists and writers. Let Africa send its students to China and its seekers after knowledge. It will not find on earth a richer goal, a more promising mine of information. On the other hand, watch the West. The new British West Indian Federation is not a form of democratic progress but a cunning attempt to reduce these islands to the control of British and American investors. Haiti is dying under rich Haitian investors who with American money are enslaving the peasantry. Cuba is showing what the West Indies, Central and South America are suffering under American big business. The American worker himself does not always realize this. He has high wages and many comforts. Rather than lose these, he keeps in office by his vote the servants of industrial exploitation so long as they maintain his wage. His labor leaders represent exploitation and not the fight against the exploitation of labor by private capital. These two sets of exploiters fall out only when one demands too large a share of the loot. This China knows. This Africa must learn. This the American Negro has failed so far to learn. I am frightened by the so-called friends who are flocking to Africa; Negro Americans trying to make money from your toil, white Americans who seek by investment at high interest to bind you in serfdom to business as the Near East is bound and as South America is struggling with. For this, America is tempting your leaders, bribing your young scholars and arming your soldiers. What shall you do?

First, understand! Realize that the great mass of mankind is freeing itself from wage slavery, while private capital in Britain, France and now in America, is still trying to maintain civilization and comfort for a few on the toil, disease and ignorance of the mass of men. Understand this, and understanding comes from direct knowledge. You know America and France and Britain to your sorrow. Now know the Soviet Union and its allied nations, but particularly know China.

China is flesh of your flesh and blood of your blood. China is colored and knows to what a colored skin in this modern world subjects its owner. But China knows more, much more than this: she knows what to do about it. She can take the insults of the United States and still hold her head high. She can make her own machines or go without machines, when America refuses to sell her American manufactures, even though it hurts American industry, and throws her workers out of jobs. China does not need American nor British missionaries to teach her religion and scare her with tales of hell. China has been in hell too long, not to believe in a heaven of her own making. This she is doing.

Come to China, Africa, and look around. Invite Africa to come, China, and see what you can teach just by pointing. Yonder old woman is working on the street. But she is happy. She has no fear. Her children are in school and a good school. If she is ill, there is a hospital where she is cared for free of charge. She has a vacation with pay each year. She can die and be buried without taxing her family to make some undertaker rich.

Africa can answer: but some of this we have done; our tribes undertake public service like this. Very well, let your tribes continue and expand this work. What Africa must realize is what China knows: that it is worse than stupid to allow a people's education to be under the control of those who seek not the progress of the people but their use as means of making themselves rich and powerful. It is wrong for the University of London to control the University of

Ghana. It is wrong for the Catholic Church to direct the education of the black Congolese. It was wrong for Protestant churches supported by British and American wealth to control higher education in China. The Soviet Union is surpassing the world in popular and higher education, because from the beginning it started its own complete educational system.

The essence of the revolution in the Soviet Union and China and in all the "iron curtain" nations, is not the violence that accompanied the change—no more than starvation at Valley Forge was the essence of the American revolution against Britain. The real revolution is the acceptance on the part of the nation of the fact that hereafter the main object of the nation is the welfare of the mass of the people and not of a lucky few.

Government is for the people's progress and not for the comfort of an aristocracy. The object of industry is the welfare of the workers and not the wealth of the owners. The object of civilization is the cultural progress of the mass of workers and not merely of an intellectual Elite. And in return for all this, communist lands believe that the cultivation of the mass of people will discover more talent and genius to serve the state than any closed aristocracy ever furnished. This belief the current history of the Soviet Union and China is proving true each day. Therefore don't let the West invest when you can avoid it. Don't buy capital from Britain, France and the United States if you can get it on reasonable terms from the Soviet Union and China. This is not politics; it is common sense. It is learning from experience. It is trusting your friends and watching your enemies.

Refuse to be cajoled or to change your way of life so as to make a few of your fellows rich at the expense of a mass of workers growing poor and sick and remaining without schools so that a few black men can have automobiles.

Africa, here is a real danger which you must avoid or return to the slavery from which you are emerging. All I ask from you is the courage to know; to look about you and see what is happening in this old and tired world; to realize the extent and depth of its rebirth and the promise which glows on yonder hills.

Visit the Soviet Union and visit China. Let your youth learn the Russian and Chinese languages. Stand together in this new world and let the old world perish in its greed or be born again in new hope and promise. Listen to the Hebrew prophet of communism:

Ho! every one that thirsteth come ye to the waters; come buy and eat, without money and without price!

Again, China and Africa, hail and farewell!

A Partial Chronology of Asia
in the Career of W. E. B. Du Bois

1885	Formation of Indian National Congress; partition of Africa at Berlin Conference
1900	Boxer Rebellion in China; first Pan-African Conference in London
1903	Publication of *Souls of Black Folk*
1904	Russo-Japanese War
1906	Publication of "The Color Line Belts the World"
1911	Attends Universal Races Congress in England
1914	World War I; publication of "The World Problem of the Color Line"
1915	Publishes "The African Roots of the War"
1917	Russian Revolution and formation of Soviet Union
1919	Publishes *Darkwater*
1921	Chinese Communist Party formed
1922	Congress of Eastern Peoples at Baku; Comintern thesis on the "Eastern Question"
1928	Publishes *Dark Princess*
1936–1937	Visits Soviet Union, Japan, Manchuria, and China; publishes "The Clash of Colour: Indians and American Negroes"
1941	U.S. enters World War II
1947	India proclaims independence; Burma proclaimed independent republic
1949	People's Republic of China formed
1957	Publishes "Will the Great Gandhi Live Again?"
1958–1959	Visits Soviet Union and China; publishes "The Vast Miracle of China Today"
1963	Joins Communist Party of the United States

Acknowledgments

The editors thank the English Departments at the University of Texas–San Antonio and Purdue University for their support for this project. They also thank Ernest Gibson for his superb editorial assistance on the manuscript. Finally, our profound gratitude to the late David Graham Du Bois. His generous, unflagging support for publication of this book is a testament to his own vision.

Index